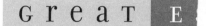

great E

D0088652

NORTHERN
CALIFORNIA

Great Escapes

Day Trips

Weekend Getaways

Easy Planning

Quick Access

Best Places to Visit

Laura Del Rosso

NORTHERN CALIFORNIA

The Countryman Press • Woodstock, Vermont

DEDICATION

In memory of my parents, Silvio and Ilva, who left everything they knew for new lives in northern California.

We welcome your comments and suggestions. Please contact Editor, The Countryman Press, P.O. Box 748, Woodstock, Vermont 05091, or e-mail countrymanpress@wwnorton.com.

ISBN 978-0-88150-783-6

Maps by Paul Woodward, © 2008 The Countryman Press
Cover and interior photos by the author unless otherwise specified
On the cover: The "espresso bus" at the Big Sur River Inn in Big Sur; the Sonoma coast from Bodega Head.
Frontispiece: Point Cabrillo Light Station in Mendocino
Book design by Bodenweber Design
Text composition by Chelsea Cloeter

Published by The Countryman Press
P.O. Box 748
Woodstock, Vermont 05091

Distributed by W. W. Norton & Company, Inc.
500 Fifth Avenue
New York, NY 10110

Printed in the United States of America

10 9 8 7 6 5 4 3 2 1

ACKNOWLEDGMENTS

Researching a book such as this can be overwhelming, and I was helped from friends who pointed me to their favorite hotels, restaurants, and hikes. Many thanks to Sharon Rooney for suggestions in Mendocino, Nina Laramore in the Russian River valley and Calistoga, Sharon Smith in west Sonoma, Julie Armstrong on the Monterey Peninsula, the Hackley family in Fort Bragg, Tina Barseghian in Oakland, Angie Di Berardino in Los Gatos, Janet Fullwood and Lucy Steffens in Sacramento, Susan Arthur in San Francisco's Mission District, Annie Wong and David Takashima for their input on Monterey eateries, John Poimiroo for his wealth of Angel Island and Yosemite knowledge, Willow Murawski-Brown in Nevada City, Annie Hellman for her Amador County and west Marin insights, and the McKenna family for their hospitality at Lake Tahoe. Special thanks go to Peter McKenna, who has meandered more of Northern California's backroads than anyone I know and whose support, wit, and sharp editing were invaluable. Encouragement came from people I met along the way, starting on my first research trip when I ran across 86-year-old Roy Daniels, in overalls, red bandana, and cowboy hat, sitting on a wooden bench at Angels Camp, offering advice on both local travel and life in general. Even the smallest of Northern California towns has a chamber of commerce or visitors center, and thanks go to their staffs, often volunteers, whose enthusiasm for their hometowns was infectious.

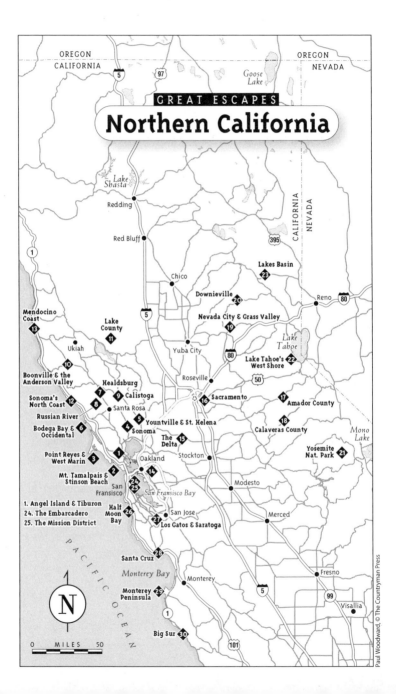

GREAT ESCAPES

Northern California

OREGON
CALIFORNIA

OREGON
NEVADA

Goose
Lake

Lake
Shasta

Redding

Red Bluff

Chico

Lakes Basin 23

Downieville 20

Nevada City & Grass Valley 19

Reno

Mendocino
Coast 13

Lake
County 11

Ukiah

Yuba City

Lake
Tahoe

Lake Tahoe's
West Shore 22

CALIFORNIA
NEVADA

Boonville & the
Anderson Valley 10

Healdsburg 7

Calistoga 9

Roseville

Sacramento 16

Amador County 17

Sonoma's
North Coast 12

Santa Rosa

8

Russian River

Yountville & St. Helena 5

Calaveras County 18

Mono
Lake

Bodega Bay &
Occidental 6

Sonoma 4

The
Delta 15

Stockton

Yosemite
Nat. Park 21

Point Reyes &
West Marin 3

Oakland

Mt. Tamalpais &
Stinson Beach 2

24

25

San
Fransisco

San Fransisco Bay

Modesto

1. Angel Island & Tiburon
24. The Embarcadero
25. The Mission District

Half
Moon
Bay

26

San Jose

Merced

Los Gatos & Saratoga 27

Santa Cruz 28

Monterey Bay

Monterey

Fresno

Monterey
Peninsula 29

Visalia

Big Sur 30

N

0   MILES   50

PACIFIC OCEAN

Paul Woodward, © The Countryman Press

CONTENTS

INTRODUCTION

For at least the last decade, studies of consumer travel behavior have tracked the shrinking American vacation and the growth of weekend getaways. These trends show no signs of slowing. More people than ever are foregoing two-week, and sometimes even their one-week vacations, and instead squeezing just a couple of days off into tight work and family schedules.

Those of us who live in Northern California count ourselves fortunate. We can travel in almost every direction and find a variety of landscapes: miles of Pacific coastline, vineyard-lined valleys, well-preserved Gold Rush towns, high mountain ranges, and vibrant cities, all well suited for quick getaways.

So maybe it's a Wednesday or maybe a Thursday evening, and you're home from work, tired but also a little restless. There is dinner to cook, bills to pay, and a pile of laundry waiting to be done. You notice your calendar is unusually free of commitments. The forecast calls for fine weather in Northern California. You think about hiking along ocean bluffs, exploring an old mining town you've heard about, sipping wine in the Dry Creek or Russian River valleys, checking out a museum in Sacramento, or lounging lazily on a Lake Tahoe shore or by a Sierra Nevada mountain river.

It's not too late to slip away. Book a flight, pack up the car, call the pet-sitter or babysitter, do whatever it takes, and head to Northern California. You could spend many days exploring here. These 30 chapters don't begin to cover all the possibilities, but, hopefully, they are a good place to start.

ABOUT *Great Escapes: Northern California*

This book is geared to people who may have only 48 hours, 24 hours, perhaps even just eight hours for a quick getaway in Northern California.

It's not designed as a comprehensive guide to the region; rather it's an assortment of possibilities. Some chapters are devoted to well-known places such as Yosemite and the Napa Valley, others are off the beaten path: Downieville, the North Sonoma Coast, and Lakes Basin, for example. Chapters on San Francisco avoid tourist areas and focus on a couple of vibrant neighborhoods where locals eat, drink, and play.

All of the destinations are within a four-hour drive of the San Francisco Bay Area and are listed geographically, according to their distance from San Francisco.

Chapters cover an area's sights, give some history, and offer suggestions for travelers who want to get out of their cars and explore on foot or by bicycle, horseback, canoe, or kayak. Most chapters have ideas for short walks or easy bike rides.

Establishments under "Where to Eat" include casual places for a quick bite and, with a nod to the growing number of foodies in America, restaurants that are renowned for fine dining. Since Northern California is the epicenter of the movement toward local and organic meat, dairy products, and produce, there's an emphasis on restaurants serving fresh, locally grown and produced food. Deli and grocery store suggestions are included as resources for picnic supplies.

Hotels and inns were chosen for each chapter's "Where to Sleep" section on the basis of their charm, uniqueness, historical significance, or good value. Their rates generally fall between $150 and $275 per room per night. Those outside of that range—hostels in San Mateo County's historic lighthouses are one example—are clearly marked as budget accommodations or, like Yosemite's Ahwahnee, for one, indicated as a splurge and included because they are one-of-a-kind experiences. Because some people don't care for the forced intimacy or regimented breakfast schedules at bed-and-breakfast inns, when a B&B is recommended, other types of accommodations are also included.

Hotels are increasingly pricing their rooms using yield management, as airlines do, so rates can fluctuate wildly depending on the season, the day of the week, or even the whim of the owner or manager. Innkeepers often cut rates for Sunday through Thursday night stays, particularly in low season. If you can take a Monday off work and stay a Sunday night, you'll not only avoid traffic congestion by starting the trip on a quiet Sunday morning, but you'll also save money. And the lower-priced spring and fall are fine times for exploring Northern California. In April and May, hills are green and the poppies bloom. In September and October, days are cooler, and there's a blaze of autumn-leaf color.

Tourist offices, always helpful, are noted under "Local Contact," and their addresses are given if they operate walk-in visitors centers. Web sites for parks, attractions, restaurants, and lodgings also are listed for more information. For more, check out www.greatescapesnorcal.com.

Use this book alone or as a jumping off point to plan your getaway, and then hit the road. Happy travels.

HEADING NORTH:
Within 100 miles of San Francisco

Castello di Amorosa, Calistoga

1 · ANGEL ISLAND & TIBURON

Tiburon is about 18 miles north of San Francisco. From US 101 north, take the Tiburon Boulevard/CA 131 exit and head east.

More than a million travelers every year visit Alcatraz, the once notorious island prison, now a national park, in San Francisco Bay. But only a fraction make it to nearby Angel Island, which, in many ways, reveals more fascinating layers of California history and offers more spectacular views.

The story of 740-acre **Angel Island** stretches well into the past. The Miwok Indians lived and fished here; a Civil War—era military base remains, along with an early 20th-century immigration station, a World War II prisoner-of-war camp, and remnants of a Cold War missile facility. In 1962, the U.S. Army decommissioned the island as a base, paving the way for its development as a state park.

Angel Island is an easy day trip from San Francisco, but getting there involves some planning. Unless you have your own boat, the way to reach it is by ferry from San Francisco, Tiburon in Marin County, or Alameda in the East Bay. The service from Alameda (510-749-5972; www.eastbay ferry.com) operates only on weekends, May through October. For ferries from San Francisco's Pier 41, check the Blue and Gold Fleet's schedules (415-773-1188; www.blueandgoldfleet.com) and plan your day accordingly; winter schedules are much reduced.

The ferry that departs from Tiburon's Main Street dock (415-435-2131; www.angelislandferry .com) is a kick—one of the last family-operated ferry services around. The second-generation owner, red-haired Maggie McDonogh, often has her kids and Labrador dog in tow as she skippers the 10-minute run, pointing out harbor seals and telling sea stories along the way.

All ferries dock at **Ayala Cove**, the island's main harbor, where the cafe serves lunch on its patio and has oysters sizzling on the barbecue. Or you can take a picnic and spread out on the large, wind-protected lawn near the visitors center. The center, in the former 1891 officers' quarters has exhibits and a 20-minute video tracing the island's history.

The fastest and easiest way to see the island is to ride the tram, which departs regularly on one-hour tours. Guided tours on Segways also are available March through November.

With 8 miles of paved trails, the island is easy and pleasant to circumnavigate by bicycle, which you may bring on any of the ferries or rent from the shops at the wharf area (see chapter 24); in Tiburon at **DemoSport** (1690 Tiburon Blvd.; 415-435-5111; www.demosport.com) on Friday, Saturday, and Sunday in summer; or from the island concessionaire (415-897-0715; www.angelisland.com).

Take the road to the left of the visitors center up a short steep hill. At the top, turn right and follow Perimeter Road, a ride of about 5 miles. For more of a workout, get off your bike when you come upon the hiking path to the summit of **Mount Livermore**, the island's 788-foot highest peak. Walk to the top and soak up the 360-degree panoramic views.

Ambitious hikers will want to take the lovely, winding **Sunset Trail** from Ayala Cove to Mount Livermore, a steep climb through groves of oak, bay, and madrone trees; this hike is especially pretty in the summer when wildflowers are in bloom. From the summit, take the North Ridge Trail back to Ayala Cove for a 5-mile loop.

There is much to explore on walks or bike rides around the island. **Camp Reynolds** is a Civil War—era fort built to protect the bay from Confederate raiders. Each June a Civil War reenactment, complete with cannons exchanging fire with a tall-masted sailing ship, brings to life that era. It's a what-if scenario: re-enactors imagine what would have happened if a Confederate vessel had come through the Golden Gate.

Another stop is the immigration station in **China Cove**, which operated from 1910 to 1940, when thousands made the long journey across the Pacific to the United

Angel Island, as seen from Marin County
ROBERT HOLMES/ CALTOUR

Walking at dusk on Angel Island

States. A moving artifact is the sad poetry carved into the walls by the Chinese immigrants detained on the island. Over 175,000 were kept here, sometimes just for hours, sometimes for weeks and months, waiting to be cleared for arrival. The station is under restoration, and, when it is reopened, picnic areas and tours of the rehabbed buildings will be available.

For another memorable experience, make Angel Island an overnight trip by staying at one of three campgrounds. You might share the island with no more than 20 other people and dozens of raccoons and deer. Backpacks are recommended because you'll need to walk a couple of miles with a tent, food, and other gear. The ridge sites (particularly campsite 4) are unforgettable sunset spots on a clear evening, when the Golden Gate Bridge and San Francisco skyline glisten. Spring and fall are the best camping periods; summer's fog and wind and winter's rain and cold can make for an unpleasant outing. The campgrounds on the island's eastern side are warmer, protected from the wind, and a better choice for summer, but the views are not as spectacular as those on the ridge. All campgrounds have running (cold) water, barbecues, and pit toilets.

Reserve them well in advance for weekends (800-444-7275; www .reserveamerica.com).

A more luxurious option is to combine Angel Island with an overnight in **Tiburon**, a destination on its own. Tiburon got its start in 1884 as a railroad town, a waterfront terminus for the San Francisco and Northwestern Pacific Railroad. But the last train left Tiburon in 1967, and the town evolved into a tony bedroom community.

A relic of the railroad past is the **Tiburon Railroad-Ferry Depot Museum** (1920 Paradise Dr.), the only surviving railroad ferry terminal west of the Hudson River. It houses a museum of local history. Upstairs is a recreated turn-of-the-nineteenth-century home, which offers a fascinating look at life in that era. Check out the **Maritime Museum** (52 Beach Rd.), made from a Victorian social saloon salvaged from a side-wheel steamer that sailed between San Francisco and the Far East; the ship was burned for scrap metal in Tiburon Cove in 1886. Both museums are open only on Sunday and Wednesday, April through October, from 1 to 4 PM. They are operated by the local Landmarks Society (415-435-1853; www.landmarks-society.org).

Some of the buildings that house the shops and galleries

along **Main Street and Ark Row** are made up of houseboats from the 1890s, when sea captains and San Franciscans had their summer floating homes here. See the building at 104 Main Street, typical of the "arks" of the period; two houseboats stacked on top of another form one home. Continue on Main Street and stroll over a bridge that connects Tiburon to Belvedere, an exclusive residential town on the tip of the Tiburon Peninsula that has some stunning mansions. Another pleasant stroll is from downtown Tiburon is about 2.8 miles along the old railroad track bed to the yellow Victorian Lyford House, part of the Richardson Bay National Audubon Center, a bird sanctuary on that sparkling cove.

A ride on the **Tiburon Peninsula Bike Loop** follows some of that same recreational trail. It starts on Paradise Drive, just steps from the ferry dock, runs along the scenic road, and cuts across the peninsula on Trestle Glen Boulevard, where it joins with the bike path at Blackie's Pasture and follows a waterfront trail back to Tiburon. It's about a 20-mile loop with some hills.

▌▌▌▌ WHERE TO EAT

For breakfast and lunch, **Sweden House Cafe** (35 Main St.; 415-435-9767) is a charming, casual eatery serving delectable buttery strudel. **Sam's Anchor Cafe** (27 Main St.; 415-435-4527; www.samscafe.com) is a mainstay, with a rowdy saloon that operated even during Prohibition; a trap door in the floor was built for access to boats hauling in whiskey. This is a prime lunch spot, offering a packed outdoor deck with killer views. **Three Degrees** (1651 Tiburon Blvd.; 415-435-3133; www.threedegrees restaurant.com), the first new restaurant to open in Tiburon in 16 years, serves California-style food. Seafood dishes are the specialty at **Guaymas** (5 Main St.; 415-4356300; www.spectrum restaurantgroup.com), an upscale Mexican restaurant that has a large selection of tequila (all shots are served with a side of a spicy tomato-citrus juice) and deck with heat lamps, allowing patrons to dine al fresco on chilly evenings.

▌▌▌▌ WHERE TO SLEEP

Water's Edge (25 Main St.; 415-789-5999, 800-738-7477; www.marinhotels.com) is a romantic luxury hotel with 23 rooms that appear to float on the bay. All rooms have fireplaces. More moderately priced is the 102-room **Lodge at Tiburon** (1651 Tiburon Blvd.; 415-435-3133, 800-762-7770; www.thelodgeat

tiburon.com), which reopened in 2006 after a massive renovation. It has an attractive New England–style décor, a library lounge with fireplace, plus a swimming pool. Bikes are provided free to guests.

■ ■ ■ ■ LOCAL CONTACT

Angel Island State Park, 415-435-1915; www.parks.ca.gov. **Tiburon Peninsula Chamber of Commerce**, 415-435-5633; www.tiburonchamber.org.

2 • MOUNT TAMALPAIS & STINSON BEACH

Mount Tamalpais is 10 miles north of San Francisco. From US 101 north, take the Stinson Beach exit. Turn left on Shoreline Highway/CA 1 and then right on Panoramic Highway.

On a clear day, the panorama from **Mount Tamalpais** is dazzling: the city of San Francisco, the bay, rolling hills, forests of fir and redwood trees, and the vastness of the Pacific. In the mornings, wisps of fog curl into its western flanks, the mountain's higher elevations poking above the white layer. In spring, lupine and poppies bloom in fields of green grass.

Most who visit Mount Tam are actually coming not for the mountain itself but for **Muir Woods National Monument** (415-388-2595; www.nps.gov /muwo) tucked into a canyon. One of the last uncut stands of ancient redwoods, it is only 12 miles north of the Golden Gate Bridge and is the closest coastal redwood forest to San Francisco. The majesty of Muir Woods outweighs its drawbacks: on summer weekends, parking and traffic congestion can create headaches; early morning visits are best. Well-marked, self-guided nature trails meander through the level valley floor of the 560-acre park, making for a pleasant stroll through the soaring redwoods. At **Cathedral Grove**, a 200-foot-tall, 12-foot-wide redwood still lies where it toppled in 1996.

Some Muir Woods trails connect to those in **Mount Tamalpais State Park** (415-388-2070; www.parks.ca.gov), which covers the rest of the sprawling mountain.

Laced with a network of hiking paths, Mount Tam has so many options that books can't cover them all. You can do a lot of exploring by car, but the best way is to venture out is on foot. Even on short, easy walks you'll be rewarded by jaw-dropping views.

Start at the Pantoll Ranger Station on Panoramic Highway and pick up a map. Everyone has a favorite hike from here, but Matt Davis Trail is hard to beat for scenery. On the gentle, level stroll of about 1½ miles along the combined Matt Davis/Coastal Trail you'll see the entire panorama. You can turn around and return to Pantoll or, for more of a challenge, veer left on Matt Davis down to Stinson Beach. Then hike back the Dipsea Trail to Steep Ravine Trail, considered to be among the most beautiful of Mount Tam's paths, for a total of 7 miles round-trip—and a 1,500-foot climb—from Pantoll.

Another hike from Pantoll, also with gorgeous views, provides a glimpse into the mountain's history. Follow the Old Mine Trail and take the spur to Cushing Memorial Theater, an outdoor amphitheater made of 4,000 stone seats and built by the Civilian Conservation Crops in the 1930s. Each June, thousands pack the place for musicals presented by a nonprofit arts association (415-383-1100; www.mountain play.org).

From the theater, take the Rock Spring Trail to the **West Point Inn** (415-646-0702; www.westpoint inn.com), which was the western-most stop of a railway known as the "Crookedest Railroad in the World" because of its 281 twists and turns from Mount Tam to the town of Mill Valley, at the mountain's base. The inn is a perfect place to kick off your boots; you can relax on the well-worn veranda and take in sweeping views. Lemonade and other refreshments are for sale in the inn's front parlor. You can also stay the night, which is fun, but the accommodations are primitive: there are no electricity or private baths, and guests must hike in (about 2 miles) with their own food and sleeping bags.

From the inn, take the Nora Trail down to Matt Davis Trail, where you'll turn right and walk through wooded and open areas back to Pantoll.

For detailed hike information, consult Pantoll rangers or the **Mount Tamalpais Interpretive Association** (415-258-2410, www .mttam.net), which conducts

Mount Tam, overlooking the Bay Area
ROBERT HOLMES/ CALTOUR

Stinson Beach and Bolinas Lagoon
PHILIP H. CLOBENTZ/ CALTOUR

regular hikes that are open to the public.

On your Mount Tam ramblings, you may think you're seeing a mirage: a colorful Alpine-style chalet that looks like it belongs in the Austrian Alps. What you're seeing is the **Nature Friends' Tourist Club** (30 Ridge Ave.; 415-388-9987), run by a hiking group with Austrian roots. Overnight stays are for members only, but anyone can enjoy the European beer on tap and the wrap-around deck with forest views. Several times a year, the club holds public festivals with polka bands, accordions, and dancing. To reach the club, make a left from Panoramic Highway onto Ridge Avenue, park at the end of the road, and walk down the paved path about a ½ mile.

At the western base of Mount Tam is **Stinson Beach**, the closest classic California beach town to San Francisco. Lifeguards are perched on duty from May to October on a wide, sandy beach that stretches more than 3 miles. A 51-acre park with more than 100 picnic sites is adjacent. Surfing is the most popular sport at Stinson, despite rare but well-publicized shark sightings. Surfboards, boogie boards, and other sports equipment can be rented at the **Live Water Surf Shop** (3448 Hwy. 1; 415-868-0333; www.livewater

surfshop.com), where the shop logo is a shark with a red X stamped over it.

Stinson Beach has never grown to more than 1,000 residents because of the twists and turns of the roads; as the crow flies, the town is close to San Francisco, but only the heartiest of people would want to commute over Mount Tam each day. The town consists of only a handful of restaurants, art galleries, and gift shops. (**Stinson Beach Books**, at 3455 Shoreline Hwy., carries a particularly good selection of local photography and children's books.)

Continue on a few miles north on CA 1 to reclusive **Bolinas**, a town famous for its attempts to remain unknown. Signs pointing to its location were torn down so often that transportation agencies have given up trying to post them. Here's the not-so-secret route: From CA 1 heading north from Stinson, take the first left after the lagoon on the Olema-Bolinas Road and then a left on Horseshoe Hill Road. A sign saying "Entering a Socially Aware, Nature-Loving Town"—no mention of Bolinas—tells you that you're going the right direction.

A haven for artists, surfers, and graying flower children, Bolinas has a short main drag that includes the Bolinas People's

Store (a community co-op) and the Spirithouse Temple, a sidewalk meditation spot dedicated to goddesses. Take a look at the **Bolinas Museum** (48 Wharf Rd.; 415-868-0330; www.bolinas museum.org) for history of the area and the work of local artists. Stroll out Wharf Road to Bolinas Beach to watch the surfers. Bolinas Beach is only a few hundred feet from Stinson Beach; the two are separated by lagoon waters.

Have a beer at **Smiley's** (41 Wharf Rd.; 415-868-1311), a tavern from the 1850s where the pool table is pushed back against the wall on Friday and Saturday nights and live bands get the crowd—aging hippies and bikers and urbanite day-trippers—rocking to the same rhythm.

▮▮▮▮ WHERE TO EAT

Parkside Cafe (43 Arenal Ave.; 415-868-1272; www.parksidecafe .com) is the only place in Stinson Beach for breakfast. The menu has plenty of choices, including omelettes with buttermilk biscuits. It's also open for lunch and dinner, and there's a to-go window for getting food for the beach. The **Stinson Beach Market** (101 Calle Del Mar; 415- 868-1923; www.stinsonbeachmarket.net) has a deli that makes sandwiches and sells picnic supplies. An old favorite for seafood and oysters is

Sand Dollar (3458 Shoreline Hwy.; 415-868-0434; www.stinson beachrestaurant.com), where the bar is a good place to relax. **Bolinas' Coast Cafe** (46 Wharf Rd.; 415-868-2298; www.bolinascafe .com) captures the town's hippie-surfer vibe with its collection of old wooden surfboards hanging on the ceiling and organic menu with vegan choices. Try the grilled oysters and salmon off the patio barbecue on summer weekends.

▮▮▮▮ WHERE TO SLEEP

On Muir Beach, just 3 miles west of Muir Woods, the **Pelican Inn** (10 Pacific Way; 415-383-6000; www.pelicaninn.com) is worth a stop for the ambiance alone. Created by a former Royal Air Force pilot as a replica of his childhood pub in England's West Country, the inn and pub features centuries-old, low doorways and fireplaces, imported from England. Overnight guests have access to the cozy, fairy-talelike living room. Room 7 under the eaves is the most popular because of its separate entrance.

The **Sandpiper Inn** in Stinson Beach (1 Marine Way; 415-868-1632; www.sandpiperstinson beach.com) is a 10-room lodge with four renovated beach cabins from the 1930s. Cabin 7 is a large room with a gas fireplace and kitchen A one-minute walk to the beach, the Sandpiper also has a lush garden with outdoor patio for enjoying the ocean air.

Mountain Home Inn (810 Panoramic Hwy.; 415-381-9000; www.mtnhomeinn.com;), perched a side of Mount Tam, is known for its bar and its restaurant's large terrace with views over the Bay Area. Of the 10 cozy rooms downstairs, five have decks with awesome views. Among them, Room 3 is the best value.

▮▮▮▮ LOCAL CONTACT

Marin County Visitors Bureau, 415-925-2060, www.visitmarin .org.

3 • POINT REYES & WEST MARIN

Point Reyes National Seashore is about 38 miles north of San Francisco. From San Francisco take US 101 north to San Anselmo/Sir Francis Drake Boulevard and follow that road west to Olema.

The **Point Reyes National Seashore**, a triangular-shaped peninsula that juts out into the Pacific Ocean, seems a remote wilderness, even though it is part of the metropolitan Bay Area.

A geologic fact adds to **Point Reyes**' otherworldliness—the peninsula is literally falling away as part of the Pacific plate creeps northwest about two inches a year and the slower North American plate travels westward. The two plates meet at the San Andreas Fault, which runs through the park entrance at the town of Olema and up Tomales Bay.

The park headquarters on Bear Valley Road, just ¼ mile west of Olema, is a good first stop. There you can get a park map and talk to the helpful staff. Point Reyes has three visitors centers, but this is the largest. It has an expansive exhibit about the natural history of the area, along with the stories of Miwoks (the local Native Americans) and explorers such as Sir Francis Drake, who sailed here in 1579. Just outside the headquarters, take a quick walk along the

Earthquake Trail; it dramatically reveals the geologic conditions at Point Reyes and how the sharp jolt of the 1906 earthquake actually shifted the peninsula 18 feet north in less than a minute.

The park, created in 1962 by President John F. Kennedy, has excellent hiking trails. Some are gentle, such as the Bear Valley Trail, which starts from the park headquarters and meanders 4.1 miles along a creek and through a forest to Arch Rock, where waves crash at steep sandstone cliffs. The Coastal Trail, which starts from the hostel off Limantour Road, is a 5-mile loop tracing the hillsides along the ocean; it can be walked in under three hours.

Binoculars come in handy for any hiking in Point Reyes. During whale migration season, particularly in April, when gray whales hug the coast to avoid predators, you have a good chance of spotting them loping through the waves.

To explore the remote reaches of the park, continue on Bear Valley Road from the headquarters past the Limantour Road turnoff, after which the road merges into Sir Francis Drake Boulevard and then passes through the town of Inverness. Then the road heads west, and after 6 miles more, you'll come across **Drake's Bay Oyster Farm** (17171 Sir Francis Drake Blvd; 415-669-1149; www .drakesbayfamilyfarms.com), operated by a fourth-generation family that raises oysters in beds here. To make sure the oysters are available to purchase when you stop by, call ahead.

A few miles further, you'll reach Drake's Beach and its visitors center with exhibits on marine life and explorers. Tall cliffs protect the long beach from the wind, so it's a fine picnic spot. The **Drake's Beach Cafe** (1 Drake's Beach Rd.; 415-669-1297; www .drakesbeachcafe.com) serves local, organic food and fish. If you're visiting on Friday and Saturday, call ahead for reservations for their twice-weekly candlelit dinners, which have become a word-of-mouth hit with the locals.

It's 6 more miles along Sir Francis Drake Boulevard to the lighthouse, a prime place for whale-watching. The 1870 structure, built low so that its beacon could shine underneath heavy fog, houses a 6,000-pound lens,

the largest of the Fresnel lenses. The beam flashed from 1870 to 1975, saving ships from wrecking on the point. Getting to the lighthouse is an adventure, because more than 300 stairs lead down to it from the visitors center, and it's a heart-pumping climb back up. The lighthouse is open every day except Tuesday and Wednesday. Call ahead (415-669-1297) to make sure it is staffed, as hours may vary and the stairs are closed when winds exceed 40 mph.

For a spectacular hike on a clear day, head for windswept **Tomales Point** at the park's northwestern edge. Take the Pierce Point Road, off Sir Francis Drake, a couple of miles north of Inverness and drive several miles past working dairy farms to the old Pierce Point farm and trailhead. This entire area is the home of dozens of Tule elk, and you'll see them roaming about. From Pierce Point farm to the ultimate point where Tomales Bay meets the Pacific is a long hike (a little over 9 miles round-trip), but it's a relatively flat trail with tranquil Tomales Bay on one side and the white-capped Pacific churning on the other side.

Tomales Bay, the narrow inlet where the San Andreas Fault runs, is often sunny, even if the coast is socked in fog. Three miles north of Inverness, in **Tomales Bay State Park**, is **Heart's Desire Beach**, a good spot for swimming and picnicking.

First-time kayakers love Tomales Bay, and paddling here often gets people hooked on the sport. You don't need much instruction (this isn't white-water kayaking that requires technique), and almost anyone can paddle the calm waters. **Blue Waters Kayaking** (415-669-2600; www.bluewaterskayaking.com) has two locations on the bay, one in Marshall on the eastern shore and one in Inverness. Venture out on your own, hire a guide, or join a group for a half- or full-day trip. You'll see harbor seals; pelicans, ospreys, and hawks; underwater oyster and kelp beds; and remote beaches. Special tours are conducted for birders, as well as those who want to stop and taste oysters or paddle under the full moon.

The main town in the area, on CA 1, 2 miles north of Olema, is charming **Point Reyes Station**. In the middle of town, the Old Western Saloon lives up to its name with a lively—some might say rowdy—vibe and unpretentious atmosphere. The town has a few shops worth a visit along its three short blocks, including Flower Power, a large household goods and gardening store, and Marty Knapp, a gallery that sells lovely black-and-white photos of the area. Don't miss Toby's, a quirky feed store, gift shop, and farm stand, and Point Reyes Books, which has a terrific collection of literature on the area and works by local authors.

▪▪▪▪ WHERE TO EAT

The national spotlight shone on Point Reyes when Britain's Prince Charles and his wife, Camilla, visited local farms in 2006. The area was already justly known in the region for its dairy products and oysters. You'll see "organic" and "local" on most menus, even at Point Reyes Station's old-fashioned **Pine Cone Diner** (60 Fourth St.; 415-663-1536), a breakfast spot with biscuits, hash, and egg dishes. To grab some lunch to take on hikes, stop at **Perry's Deli** (12301 Sir Francis Drake Blvd.; 415-663-1491) in Inverness Park, a few miles north of park headquarters, for sandwiches and locally made bread. (Breadmaiden of Point Reyes Station is one provider.) Or, in Point Reyes Station, get pastries, bread, or a cup of organic coffee at **Bovine Bakery** (11315 Hwy. 1; 415-663-9420), the kind of place where regulars store their coffee mugs on a shelf. More lunch fixin's can be bought at a renovated hay barn known as **Tomales Bay Foods**, home of

Cowgirl Creamery (80 Fourth St.; 415-663-9335; www.cowgirl creamery.com); the creamery makes northern California's most famous cheeses, such as Red Hawk, a triple cream cheese, from West Marin's dairy cows. **Station House Cafe** (11180 Hwy. 1; 415-663-1515; www.stationhousecafe .com) has a pretty patio for dining and serves up American comfort food. The **Olema Inn** (10,000 Sir Francis Drake Blvd.; 415-663-9559; www.theolemainn.com), with its romantic white tablecloth—style dining in an 1876 roadhouse and menu of local mussels, oysters, and other fish or Sonoma pheasant, is the place for an elegant dinner. Six lovely rooms upstairs have Ralph Lauren linens and high-end European mattresses. In mid-2006, the long-awaited **Nick's Cove** (23240 Hwy. 1; 415-663-1033; www.nicks cove.com) opened on the east side of Tomales Bay, in the hamlet of Marshall. The rustic old buildings have been renovated into a casual fish restaurant, which, not surprisingly, focuses on oysters and fish in season.

▮▮▮▮ WHERE TO SLEEP

The **Bear Valley Inn** (Hwy. 1 at Bear Valley Rd.; 415-663-1777; www.bearvinn.com) is the closest accommodation to park headquarters. Rates are reasonable, and there's a homey atmosphere with lots of family artwork on the walls and step-up beds. At Inverness's **Blackthorne Inn** (266 Vallejo Ave.; 415-663-8621; www .blackthorneinn.com), proprietors Susan and Bill Wigert are the area's pioneer bed-and-breakfast owners. Their whimsical lodge is topped by the Eagle's Nest, an octagonal-shaped room perched amid the trees above the inn (the bathroom on an adjacent deck, however). Ask Bill for stories on how he built the stone fireplace and nabbed an old San Francisco train station entrance door for use as a deck door. **Ten Inverness Way** (10 Inverness Way; 415-669-1648; www.teninversness way.com) is run by Teri Mattson, who calls it "the inn for hikers and readers." Rooms at this 1904 Craftsman home, built right along Inverness Creek, are small (except for the suite), and the bathrooms show their age, but the warmth of the large great room and its big fireplace, the cozy library, and inviting back patio make up for the drawbacks. When booking, ask about complimentary guest excursions, such as bonfires on Point Reyes beaches, which take place several times per year. The most pricey of the Point Reyes inns is the newest, the four-room **Olema Druids Hall** (9870 Shoreline Hwy.; 415-663-8727; 866-554-4255; www.olemadruidshall.com). The inn's stylishly renovated 1885 building—think a millionaire's beach home in the Hamptons—was a meeting hall of a fraternity-like society of local farmers and ranchers. (The Druids' bizarre ephemera are on display in the living room.) The Nest room is the best value, and its bed is sumptuous, with down comforters and high-thread-count sheets.

▮▮▮▮ LOCAL CONTACT

Point Reyes National Seashore, 415-464-5100, www.nps.gov/pore.

4 · THE TOWN OF SONOMA

Sonoma is 55 miles north of San Francisco. From US 101 north, take CA 37 east and a left on CA 121 toward Sonoma. Turn left onto CA 12 to reach the town.

The 16-mile long Sonoma Valley, with its neat rows of grape vines between the Sonoma and Mayacamas mountains, is the historical center of the California wine industry and the founding of the state. It was the home of two intriguing men: Hungarian count Agostin Haraszthy, who first planted grapes in the valley in 1851, and former Mexican general Mariano Vallejo, later a state politician, grape grower, and rancher, who wrote his five-volume history of California here.

The historic town plaza is the heart of **Sonoma**. A shady, lovely park, the plaza, until a few years ago, kept its farm town past alive with a flock of clucking chickens who roamed the square. They were removed in 2000, a controversy that still ignites pro-chicken and antichicken passions. This plaza is a perfect place to stroll, with its combination of historic buildings, restaurants and cafes, and high-end shops. The latter include **Summervine** (100 Spain St. W.), selling unique household goods, and **Baksheesh** (423 First

St. W.), which sells items made by Third World artisans. The **Sonoma Cheese Factory** (2 Spain St.) is a bit touristy, but fun, and a good spot to stock up on picnic supplies.

On the northeastern corner of the plaza are several complexes that make up the **Sonoma State Historic Park** (363 Third St. W.; 707-938-9560; www.parks.ca .gov). Mission San Francisco Solano de Sonoma, the northernmost and last mission built in California, dates from 1823. The **Sonoma Barracks**, built of adobe brick and wood in 1841, was the headquarters of *Commandante* Vallejo, who was ordered to move his company from San Francisco north to Sonoma as a buffer against potential Russian movement from Fort Ross on the coast. It wasn't used as a barracks for very long. In 1860, after California was admitted to the union, Vallejo remodeled the building to be a winery.

Exhibits at the visitors center describe mission life and the history of the Bear Flag Revolt, in which a group of American settlers "arrested" Vallejo and raised the California flag for the first time, proclaiming California a free republic. The revolt lasted only 25 days, when a U.S. Navy officer—the grandson of Paul Revere—came to town and replaced the flag with the Stars and Stripes. Look for the bronze statue on the northern corner of the plaza, commemorating the event site.

An easy 10-minute walk outside of the plaza (the path is just in back of the Sonoma Barracks) is Vallejo's Gothic-style home, **Lachryma Montis**, or "Tears of the Mountain," named for the spring behind the house. The parlor, furnished with a French-imported rosewood piano, and an impressive library that was reportedly the largest in California, give a flavor of Vallejo's full life (he and his wife had 16 children). One entrance fee covers the Sonoma State Historic Park's Sonoma Barracks, the mission, and the Vallejo house.

Behind the Sonoma Barracks is another historical venue, the volunteer-run **Depot Park Museum**. Housed in an old train station, the museum relates the story of rail transportation in the wine country. Among the exhibits of regional history is a wall-sized painting depicting the Bear Flat Revolt. Admission is free.

Sonoma is a quiet town, but there is nightlife at **Murphy's Irish Pub** (464 First St. E.; 707-935-0660; www.sonomapub.com), with live music Thursday through Sunday nights and a large selection of draft beers and ales. On Tuesday evenings from April through October, a farmers' market, with arts and craft vendors, as well as produce sellers, enlivens the plaza from 5:30 PM to dusk. There is also a Friday-morning market in the plaza year-round.

Two wineries within a five-minute drive of the plaza are among the most historic in the state: the **Buena Vista Winery** (18000 Old Winery Rd.; 707-265-1472; wwwbuenavistacarneros.com), a designated historic landmark founded by Haraszthy, and **Sebastiani** (389 Fourth St. E.; 800-888-5532; www.sebastiani.com), the oldest continuous family-owned winery in California. Follow little white arrows to a dozen or more others in the area, including some small places such as **Bartholomew Park Winery** (1000 Vineyard Ln.; 707-935-9511; www.bartholomewparkwinery.com). Tucked away in the eastern hills, this historic locale has beautiful gardens and a museum where you can learn some intriguing history involving female convicts and 200 Angora cats that once occupied the place. Three miles of hiking trails and picnic grounds make it a favorite. Or skip driving, stay in town, and sample a large selection of local wines on the plaza at the **Wine Exchange of Sonoma** (452 First St. E.; 707-938-1704; www.wineexsonoma.com), a favorite of locals.

The town of **Glen Ellen** is about 6 miles north of the plaza. Set along Sonoma Creek, it was the home of the late, great food writer M. F. K. Fisher, who chose to live in the area because of its many similarities to her beloved France. Glen Ellen also is associated with writer and adventurer Jack London, whose ranch makes up **Jack London State Historic Park** (2400 London Ranch Rd.; 707-938-5216; www.parks.ca .gov). On a walk around the park's wooded grounds you'll see a lake, a boathouse, and the ruins of Wolf House, London's dream home of redwood and local stone.

Tragically, it burned down in 1913, just weeks before he and his wife, Charmain, were to move in. Still standing is the stone-walled House of Happy Walls, built by Charmain after London's death in 1916. Today it's a visitors center and small museum displaying London's typewriter and furnishings for Wolf House. A gift shop sells London's books.

You can tour the park by walking the trails or, as London preferred, by horse. **Triple Creek Horse Outfit** (707-887-8700; www.triplecreekhorseoutfit.com) offers one- and two-hour rides April though October. The company also conducts horseback rides of **Sugarloaf Ridge State Park**, about 15 minutes north of Sonoma.

A beautiful, short drive from Sonoma or Glen Ellen is bucolic **Kenwood**, the home of several renowned wineries. **Chateau St. Jean** (8555 Sonoma Hwy; 707-833-4134; www.chateaustjean

Mission San Francisco de Solano, Sonoma

General Mariano Vallejo's home, Sonoma

.com) has gardens, a gourmet deli, and, among the vineyards, a large lawn with tables for picnicking.

▮▮▮▮ WHERE TO EAT

Sonoma's plaza area is full of a range of restaurants, from casual to elegant. **Basque Boulangerie** (460 First St. E.; 707-935-7687) is the locals' place for breakfast and quick lunch, with flaky cheese danish and a big selection of sandwiches. **The Sunflower Caffe** (421 First St. W.; 707-996-6645) in Vallejo's first Sonoma home, a 19th-century adobe, is a laid-back spot for breakfast and delicious coffee that you can sip on a pretty garden patio. **The Girl and the Fig** (110 W. Spain St.; 707-938-3634; www.thegirlandthefig.com) offers classic French home-style cooking. **The Red Grape** (529 First St. W.; 707-996-4103; www.thered grape.com) is a casual and inexpensive pizza-and-pasta place. More upscale is **El Dorado Kitchen** (405 First St. W; 707-996-3030; www.eldoradosonoma.com), which has a lovely patio and acclaimed California-Italian food. **Cafe La Haye** (140 E. Napa St.; 707-935-5994; www.cafelahaye .com), a tiny casually elegant spot, serves delicious California cuisine amid artwork whose creators have their studios next door at the La Haye Art Center.

▮▮▮▮ WHERE TO SLEEP

The Sonoma Valley has a large selection of accommodations. As in other wine-country areas, rates climb during the September and October harvest season and midweek rates are much lower than weekends, when a two-night minimum is often required.

Glenelly Inn (5131 Warm Springs Rd., Glen Ellen; 707-996-6720; www.glenelly.com), an inn since 1916, today is run by Kristi Jeppesen, who once lived in Norway. That influence is obvious, with beds covered in Norwegian down comforters and Scandinavian-style breakfast served by a beautiful old cobblestone fireplace. Some of the rooms are on the small side, but they are a good value and have private entrances.

Tuscan-style **Bungalows 313** (313 First St. E.; 707-996-8091; www.bungalows313.com), just off Sonoma's plaza, is more pricey, but luxurious. Six stylishly appointed rooms have fine linens, kitchens, and private patios.

The Sonoma Chalet (18935 Fifth St. W.; 707-938-3129, 800-938-3129; www.sonomachalet .com) looks like the house of a friend you wish you had in the wine country, with its Oriental rugs on well-worn wooden floors, antique stoves and wood-burning fireplaces, stacks of books and magazines, and lots of places to curl up and read. The turn-of-the-19th-century main house has four rooms; three rustic and charming cottages are scattered on the grounds.

The **El Pueblo Inn** (896 Napa St. W.; 707-996-3651, 800-900-8844); www.elpuebloinn.com), about ½ mile off the plaza, is a family-run, up-market motel that has landscaped gardens and pool area. For just a few dollars more you can upgrade to a newer room with patios or balconies. There is no two-night minimum on weekends, but you should book weeks in advance for high season.

■ ■ ■ ■ LOCAL CONTACT

Sonoma Valley Visitors Bureau, visitors center on the plaza, 453 First St. E; 707-996-1090, 866-996-1090; www.sonomavalley.com.

5 • YOUNTVILLE & ST. HELENA

Yountville is about 55 miles from San Francisco. Take US 101 north or I-80 East to CA 37 and follow the signs to Napa and CA 29, which leads to Yountville.

A few years ago the travel industry identified an emerging trend that it named "culinary tourism": people traveling primarily for the food. Nowhere is that phenomenon more alive than in **Yountville** and **St. Helena**, two Napa Valley towns that in the 1970s and 1980s became renowned for wine but are now also must destinations for foodies.

Napa Valley gets 4.7 million visitors a year, and on summer weekends or during the fall harvest, the main artery through Yountville and St. Helena, two-lane CA 29, seems anything but a peaceful country road. Try to visit on weekdays or during the off season, or else stick to the Silverado Trail on the valley's eastern side.

Yountville used to be a quiet residential town mainly known for its veterans' home, the largest in the western United States and established in 1884 by veterans of the Mexican and Civil wars; a majority of the town's residents, veterans of more recent conflicts, still live at the home. But a change came to Yountville in 1994: Chef Thomas Keller chose a handsome old stone building (once a laundry) and created one of the most acclaimed American restaurants, the French Laundry. Others chefs followed suit, and today the town has a row of restaurants that have become destinations (see "Where to Eat").

Pick up a walking-tour map at the visitors center (see "Local Contact") and hike the mostly level, 5-mile Yount Mill Loop trail, stopping at several sites listed on the National Register of Historic Places, such as the former Groezinger Winery, established in 1870. Today it's the centerpiece of Vintage 1870, a retail complex that includes Blue Heron Gallery, which features works by local artists. The path also leads by the veterans' home, whose chapel was built in 1871, and, nearby, the **Napa Valley Museum** (55 Presidents Cir.; 707-944-0500; www.napavalleymuseum.org), which describes valley history and winemaking through interactive displays.

North of Yountville, CA 29 becomes Main Street, St. Helena. Though the town was once the hub of an agricultural valley, its merchants today are more likely to sell Italian cashmere sweaters than hoes and rakes. Four blocks are lined with luxury shops purveying fine apparel, housewares, and specialty foods. One such shop is **Jan de Luz** (1219 Main St.), a Provençal household-goods store with beautiful linens; another is **St. Helena Olive Oil Company** (1351 Main St.), which resides in an 1882 bank building and features a lovely, original pressed-tin ceiling.

Even nonfoodies will enjoy a stop at the **Culinary Institute of America (CIA) at Greystone** (2555 Main St.; 707-967-2320; www.cia chef.edu); in the building that housed the largest stone winery in the world when it opened in 1889. From the 1950s until 1989, it was the Christian Brothers Winery. Take the self-guided tour and check out one of the hour-long cooking demonstrations, the 3,000-square-foot gift shop, and Brother Timothy's collection of 1,500 antique corkscrews. You may want to dine on the terrace at the Wine Spectator Greystone restaurant, where the food is cooked and served by CIA students.

The visitors centers in both St. Helena and Yountville (see "Local Contact") are good first stops before heading out for wine tasting. Volunteers help sort out the overwhelming choices of wineries—more than 400—based on your interest and level of knowledge. They also have coupons for discounts on tasting fees. Don't be put off when winery listings say, "Tasting by appointment only." Often you can call just a couple of hours ahead (an ideal use for cell phones as you're driving around the valley) and find a spot for a private tour and tasting, a more personal and memorable experience than a typical group tour.

Vine Cliff (7400 Silverado Tr.; 707-944-1364; www.vinecliff.com) is one such winery offering appointment-only tastings. Tucked in a quiet canyon and established in the late 1880s, it has 150,000 square feet of caves and a lovely tasting room in which to sample its cabernet sauvignon and chardonnay. Since the first days of winemaking, underground caves have been used to keep fermentation at a steady temperature. Other Napa-area wineries including landmark **Beringer** (2000 Main St.; 707-963-8989; www.beringer .com), offer cave tours. The Beringer caves, some of the oldest in the valley, were carved in the 1880s by Chinese laborers working by candlelight; the caves still maintain a perfect 58-degree temperature.

For an example of a small, family-owned winery, unpretentious and fun to visit, try **Goosecross** (1119 State Ln.; 707-944-1986; www.goosecross.com). Some call this the rock 'n' roll winery due to the music usually playing on the stereo system and the spunky young wine pourers leading the tastings. The larger wineries also are well worth a visit. Yountville's **Domaine Chandon** (1 California Dr.; 707-944-2280; www.chandon.com) has a 45-minute tour that focuses on the fermentation particular to sparkling wines. Its tasting room, with a menu of delicious charcuterie and sandwiches, is also a good place for a light lunch. One of the leaders of the California wine industry, **Robert Mondavi** (Hwy. 29, Oakville; 888-766-6328; www.mondavi.com), with its graceful Mediterranean-style architecture, signature tower, and courtyards, offers 75-minute tours that take visitors from the vineyard to the cellars.

Olive oil production is growing here. At **Artesa Round Pond** in Rutherford (886 Rutherford Rd.; 707-963-7555; www.roundpond .com), a large, gleaming Italian olive-crushing machine produces oil from the estate's trees. A tasting room offers sips of the local oils. For a more funky olive oil experience and a retro flavor of Napa Valley, head to an old barn in St. Helena where the **Napa Valley Olive Oil Manufacturing Company** (835 Charter Oak; 707-963-4173) sells picnic supplies and oil made from Central Valley olives in cavelike rooms that are covered with thousands of customers' business cards.

If you fancy having someone else do the driving on your wine-tasting travels through the valley, several companies offer services. One is the **Napa Valley Winery Shuttle** (707-257-1950; www.wine shuttle.com), which charges $60 for the day. You'll be on board with eight to 10 other people, visit five to six wineries, and get picked up and dropped off at your hotel.

Bicycling is another way to see Napa Valley. Several cross-valley roads run through vineyards so that you can avoid the traffic on CA 29. Pick up maps at the visitors centers or at bike shops. In Yountville, **Napa Valley Bike Tours** (6488 Washington St.; 707-944-2953; www.napavalleybike tours.com) offers guided tours as well as bicycle rentals. In St. Helena, try **St. Helena Cyclery** (1156 Main St.; 707-963-7736; www.sthelenacyclery.com). A gentle 25-mile loop leads from

Domaine Chandon winery, Yountville

Sweets at the Bouchon Bakery, Yountville

the shop along Dry Creek Road north to the Oakville grade and back to St. Helena.

Almost every morning the skies of Napa Valley host a colorful sight: an array of hot air balloons drifting quietly in the still of the dawn. The sunrise trips, which depend on local weather conditions, last about an hour and are available through several companies, including **Napa Valley Balloons** (800-253-22244; 707-944-0228; www.napavalleyballoons.com) and **Adventures Aloft** (800-944-4408; www.napavalleyaloft.com)

▪▪▪▪ WHERE TO EAT

Along Washington Street, Yountville's restaurant row, Thomas Keller's **Bouchon** (6534 Washington St.; 707-944-8037; www.frenchlaundry.com) is a red-burgundy bistro serving classics such as steak and *pommes frites* and a raw seafood bar. Reservations are easier to come by here than at the chef's more

famous restaurant. Next door, the **Bouchon Bakery** (6528 Washington St.; 707-944-2253) has delectable French-style pastries and rustic breads. Two restaurants require some prior effort to get a table. One is the acclaimed **Redd** (6480 Washington St.; 707-944-2222; www.reddnapavalley.com); dinner reservations usually need to be made six weeks in advance. However, you can often get a lunch table at Redd without reservations, and the menu selections, including a tasting menu, are similar to the dinner selections. There's also a full bar open until 11:30 PM with a bar menu. And then there's the **French Laundry** (6640 Washington St.; 707-944-2380; www.frenchlaundry.com), where dinner for two, without wine, typically runs about $500. Reservations are snapped up two months in advance, on the day the books open.

In St. Helena's **Go Fish** (641 Main St.; 707-963-0700; www.gofishrestaurant.net), chef Cindy

Pawlcyn, known for Napa Valley's Mustards Grill, has garnered raves for her fresh fish, served sautéed, wood-grilled, or poached. However, you don't have to spend a lot to eat well in St. Helena. Try local institution and favorite **Taylor's Automatic Refresher** (933 Main St.; 707-963-3486; www.taylorsrefresher.com), a classic hamburger stand, except this one, not surprisingly, serves wine. It's the toasted egg buns that make the burgers a treat. **Oakville Grocery** (7856 Hwy. 29; 707-944-8802; www.oakvillegrocery.com), in operation since 1881, is another standby for gourmet picnic supplies, including breads from the valley's fine bakers.

▪▪▪▪ WHERE TO SLEEP

It can be difficult to find a place in the Napa Valley for less than $300 a night, except in the November through March low season. But several hotels, including three in Yountville within walking distance of the town's famous restaurants, fit the bill, with rooms under $275.

    Lavender (2020 Webber St.; 707-944-1399; 800-522-4140; www.foursisters.com) has the style of a French country inn. Several spacious rooms have private patios. Guests have use of bicycles, and evening receptions often include wine tasting with a

local winemaker. A sister inn is **Maison Fleurie** (6529 Yount St.; 707-944-2056; www.maisonfleurienapa.com), which has a lovely pool area and a main house in a picturesque historic stone building. **The Napa Valley Railway Inn** (6523 Washington St.; 707-944-2000; www.napavalleyrailwayinn.com) offers colorful renovated railcars, including surprisingly spacious and lovely cattle cars and cabooses, as overnight lodging at good rates. Just outside of St. Helena is a longtime favorite, **El Bonita** (195 Main St.; 707-963-3216; www.elbonita.com), originally a motor inn from the 1950s (the old neon sign is one of the few '50s relics along CA 29). Choose rooms in the Homestead building, some of which have private patios. The decor is simple and unpretentious, the place is well maintained, and the gardens are pretty.

▪▪▪▪ LOCAL CONTACT

Yountville Chamber of Commerce, visitors center at 6484 Washington St.; 707-944-0904, www.yountville.com. **St. Helena Chamber of Commerce**, visitors center at 1010 Main St.; 800-799-6456; www.sthelena.com. **Napa Valley Conference and Visitors Bureau**, visitors center at 1310 Napa Town Center, Napa; 707-226-7459; www.napavalley.org.

6 • BODEGA BAY & OCCIDENTAL

Bodega Bay is about 67 miles from San Francisco. Take US 101 north to the Central Petaluma exit and follow the signs to Bodega Bay, taking Bodega Avenue, which becomes Valley Ford Road. After 28 miles, the road merges

onto CA 1. Head north to town.

Bodega Bay isn't a traditional town; there's no center, really—only houses, hotels, wharfside restaurants, and shops bordering a couple of miles of CA 1. All businesses overlook a large, natural harbor where fishing boats bring in their catch: prized Dungeness crab in winter and wild salmon in summer.

Named after a Spanish explorer, Francisco de la Bodega y Quadra, who took refuge here in 1775 after running afoul of nasty currents off Point Reyes, Bodega Bay was settled in due course by Russians, Mexicans, and a New England sea captain, Stephen Smith, who owned the land in the mid-19th century. The town did not thrive, however, until the 1940s, when the narrow channel between bay and ocean was dredged and commercial fishing expanded.

Other than its fishing fleet, Bodega Bay's claim to fame is as the setting of Alfred Hitchcock's horror flick *The Birds*, filmed in 1962. More than 40 years later, several filming locations remain and still draw movie buffs. The visitors center (see "Local Contact") has directions to the settings.

To get a sense of the area's geography, from CA 1 a mile south of town, turn at Doran Beach Road and head to **Doran Beach Regional Park** (201 Doran Beach Rd.; 707-875-3540; www.co.sonoma.ca.us). Stroll the wide, 2-mile strand along a curvy spit that separates Bodega harbor from the bay, while the imposing bluffs of Bodega Head tower to the west. You'll hear a cacophony of sea lions barking from **Bodega Rock** offshore.

Back on CA 1, check out the **Tides Wharf** (835 Hwy. 1), an oyster and snack bar, gift shop, restaurant, and fish market perched along the bay. The original Tides was featured in *The Birds*, but it later burned, and the complex was rebuilt. Among the other worthwhile stops are the **Ren Brown Collection** (1781 Hwy. 1), a lovely gallery with Japanese artwork and more, and **Gourmet au Bay** (913 Hwy. 1), a wine tasting room that includes a heated deck with water views.

To explore **Bodega Head**, go a mile north of town on CA 1, take a left on Eastshore Road, a right on Bay Flat Road, and continue 3 miles, passing the marina and a couple of roadside ponds that attract egrets, pelicans, sandpipers, and other shorebirds and waterfowl. The biggest birding spot in Sonoma County, the bay lies on the Pacific Flyway and draws migratory birds—not nearly as menacing as Hitchcock's depiction—as they take a breather on their way south for the winter. Late August through October is the peak of the migration, but plenty of varieties are here year-round.

At the **Campbell Cove** beach and picnic area, a wooden walkway leads to "**the Hole in the Head**," the remnant of the foundation for a nuclear power plant proposed by Pacific Gas and Electric in 1960. The project was stopped by local residents and antinuclear activists, who were helped in their argument by a simple fact—the spot isn't the most ideal location for a nuclear plant: the San Andreas Fault runs under Bodega Bay. The 192-foot deep foundation, however, was already dug. Not much is left except for the "hole," which is now part of the state park at Bodega Head and a reminder of a project that would have dramatically altered Bodega Bay.

Continue driving on the road uphill from Campbell Cove to the parking lot and overlook on Bodega Head, surrounded on three sides by water: the Pacific Ocean to the west, the harbor and its narrow entrance to the bay on the south and east. Sea lions and seals flop around the rocks year round. In winter, it's a prime spot to watch the gray-whale migration.

From the overlook you can walk

Bodega Bay harbor

View north from Bodega Head

1½ miles on a loop around Bodega Head; be careful not to get too close to the sheer cliffs. Remember to pack a windbreaker or sweater: it's breezy, cool, and often foggy here. On a clear day, the dramatic north Sonoma coastline stretches northward, and, to the south, the Point Reyes peninsula can be seen. Atop the windswept bluff stands a stark memorial to local fishermen who lost their lives in area waters.

You can also walk from the parking lot north on the Overlook/Salmon Creek Trail. At about ½ mile, a junction offers trails to the left and right. To the left, a short path leads to the stunning overlook at Horseshoe Cove. To the right, the trail leads across the **University of California Davis Bodega Marine Lab** property and through tall sand dunes to Salmon Creek Beach—a round-trip hike of about 4 miles.

The lab (707-875-2211; www.bml.ucdavis.edu) is open for two-hour drop-in tours on Friday between 2 and 4 PM. Visitors can see aquariums full of local underwater life and learn about the geology of the area and the lab's ongoing research.

Both Campbell Cove and Doran Park are accessible by relatively flat, easy bicycle rides. **Bodega Bay Surf Shack** (1400 Hwy. 1; 707-875-3944; www.bodegabaysurf.com) rents bicycles, plus kayaks for exploring the bay or local estuaries and rivers.

One mile north of town along CA 1 is **Chanslor Ranch** (707-875-333; www.chanslor.com), where you can join an organized, hour-and-a-half horseback ride to nearby beaches several times a day—outings designed for those with little riding experience. The stable also conducts private rides for parties of two. Call for reservations.

Heading north about a mile from Chanslor is **Salmon Creek Beach**, a gorgeous white-sand beach lined with dunes and dotted with driftwood. It's popular with surfers, walkers, and picnickers.

The tiny town of **Bodega**, 5 miles south and inland of Bodega Bay (take CA 1 and then head east on Bodega Highway), will be familiar from *The Birds*: St. Teresa of Avila Church is the picturesque, white-steepled landmark, built on the hill in 1860. Behind it is the Potter School, which figured in the movie; teacher Suzanne Pleshette and her pupils were attacked by ravens here. Now a private residence, the Taylor family runs a small gift shop inside, open on weekends, with movie memorabilia and local-history books. For a pick-me-up, make sure to stop by **Brew** (17192

Bodega Hwy.), a tiny coffee-house—really only a wooden shack. The front porch is a pleasant spot to watch the comings and goings of the town, which in reality are a good deal less terrifying than in Hitchcock's movie.

From Bodega continue east on Bodega Road, then making a left on the Bohemian Highway to the equally tiny burg of **Freestone. Wild Flour Bread** (140 Bohemian Hwy., 707-874-2938; www.wild flourbread.com) has a baker's dozen variety of crusty breads, sticky buns, and scones made from organic flour in a wood-fired brick oven. Outside, there's a garden open for a look about.

Freestone is well known among spa-goers as home of **Osmosis** (209 Bohemian Hwy.; 707-823-8231; www.osmosis.com). It's the only spa in the U.S. that specializes in soothing and energizing Japanese enzyme baths, made up of finely milled cedar and Douglas fir, rice bran, and 600 plant enzymes. Guests also relax in tranquil gardens of bonsai and bamboo by the koi pond.

Just 4 miles north of Freestone is the village of **Occidental**, a pleasant little place dating from the 1870s and nestled in a sunny, redwood-forested canyon. Occidental is a destination for day-trippers, who come for lunch or dinner at its restaurants (see

"Where to Eat") and to amble around the shops on its five blocks. Friday evenings, from 4 PM through dusk, June through October, the town hums with a local farmers' market featuring local produce, meats, fish, and crafts.

From Occidental, make a loop back to Bodega Bay by continuing on Bohemian Highway north to Monte Rio (see chapter 8) and then turning west on CA 116, reconnecting to CA 1 south at Jenner.

If you're driving back to the Bay Area from Bodega Bay, you'll return on CA 1 south, which merges onto Valley Ford Road, passing a procession of dairies, ranches, and weather-beaten wooden barns—a pastoral delight in spring when the hills are a lush green and the poppies bloom. This route was the main Indian trail from Bodega to the inland valleys and was marked by a plaque at **Two Rock**, the juncture of several Mexican land grants.

The hamlet of **Valley Ford**, an old stop for a narrow-gauge railroad that hauled lumber, dairy, and farm goods to San Francisco, includes a hotel, restaurants (see "Where to Sleep" and "Where to Eat"), and Valley Ford Market, an old-fashioned deli stocked with smoked salmon and sausages made by the owner.

▪▪▪▪ WHERE TO EAT

People drive for miles to dine at Bodega Bay's **Seaweed Cafe** (1580 Eastshore Rd.; 707-875-2700; www.seaweedcafe.com), part of the "slow food" movement dedicated to local, organic ingredients. It's only open for dinner Thursday through Sunday and brunch on Sunday. Nearby, on the harbor, is **Sandpiper** (1410 Bay Flat Rd.; 707-875-2278; www.sandpiperrestaurant.com), a low-key locals' hangout where jazz and Willie Nelson are the background music and where a knock-out clam chowder is the specialty.

In Occidental, **Howard Station Cafe** (3611 Main St.; 707-874-2838; www.howardstationcafe.com), which everyone calls Howard's, is a homey spot that serves big breakfasts and burgers and vegetarian dishes for lunch. Nearby, the **Union Hotel** (3731 Main St.; 707-874-3555; www.unionhotel.com), a historic restaurant from 1879, offers several options: a saloon, a family-style Italian eatery with multi-course feasts, a pizza parlor, and a casual coffeehouse with adjoining patio for a quick lunch—all run by the same family who started the operation five generations ago. **Bistro Des Copains** (3782 Bohemian Hwy.; 707-874-2436; www.bistrodescopains

.com), a newish, dinner-only restaurant, is a slice of France. Roast lamb and grilled wild salmon are the menu stars. On Tuesday, there's no corkage fee for Sonoma County wines.

Rocker Oysterfeller's in the Valley Ford Hotel (14415 Hwy. 1, Valley Ford; 707-876-1983; www.ffrsi.com) has a zesty, Southern-influenced menu that uses local oysters, fish, lamb, and other ingredients. The cheese plates include selections from, among others, Bellwether Farms just up the road. The restaurant's bar and outdoor patio are hoppin' with live music on weekend nights, but bands play only until about 9 PM so that hotel guests (see "Where to Sleep") aren't kept up.

▪▪▪▪ WHERE TO SLEEP

The **Bodega Bay Lodge** (103 Hwy. 1; 707-875-3525, 888-875-3525; www.bodegabaylodge.com), a luxurious, wood-shingled hotel with a full-service spa, overlooks the ocean and harbor. Second-floor rooms with balconies have beautiful views and are worth the extra price. Look for midweek specials and spa packages for good rates.

The **Bodega Bay Inn** (1588 Eastshore Rd.; 888-875-8733; www.bodegabayinn.com) is a funky artist's house transformed into a small inn and art gallery by owner Ruth Branscomb and her son, Ed Dechant. Room 7, with its large terrace and private entrance, is a good value. There are no ocean views, but the lovely garden in the back and the sunroom where a continental breakfast is served are relaxing spots.

Valley Ford Hotel (see Rocker Oysterfeller's under "Where to Eat") was built in 1864 and restored in the last few years. Six rooms are simply but comfortably decorated and have luxurious bed linens. The two rooms facing the highway have some road noise.

The Inn at Occidental (3657 Church St.; 707-874-1047, 800-522-6324; www.innatoccidental.com), dating from 1877, has been a modern lodge since 1988. Rooms are large and decorated with colorful quilts and quirky antiques; the Kitchen Cupboard Room has a charming display of old kitchen gadgets. All rooms have gas fireplaces and cozy sitting areas. It's not a budget choice: the Leaf Umbrella, Sugar, and Ivory rooms are under $275, but the others are over $325.

▦▦ LOCAL CONTACT

Sonoma Coast Visitors Center at 850 CA 1 in Bodega Bay, 707-875-3866, www.bodegabay.com.

7 · HEALDSBURG

Healdsburg is about 70 miles north of San Francisco. Take US 101 north to the exit for central Healdsburg.

Healdsburg's transformation from sleepy agricultural community to an upscale travel destination happened so quickly that old-timers are still taken aback by the changes. Ray Lewand, the owner of the Camellia Inn, one of the town's first bed-and-breakfast inns, remembers when city leaders tried to interest developers in sprucing up the town plaza to attract tourism 20 years ago: "They told us to forget it because nobody had ever heard of Healdsburg." How things change.

Most trace the start of the transformation to the openings of famed chef Charlie Palmer's restaurant, Dry Creek Kitchen, and the stylish Hotel Healdsburg in 2001, which gave the town national attention. Since then, the plaza was renovated, and the area boomed with more and more chic apparel and household boutiques, wine-tasting rooms, and art galleries. The entire downtown is an enjoyable place to spend time. You can linger at one of many coffeehouses (**Flying Goat** at 324 Center St. is the locals' hangout), shop, stop at the tasting rooms, and have a meal at one of the fine restaurants.

The plaza is also the scene of a bustling Tuesday evening farmers' market (4 to 8 PM), which features standing-room-only concerts from May through August. The events are so popular that the organizers imposed strict rules about when you can lay down your lawn blankets (not until 4 PM).

To get a feel for the history of the area and how it went from growing hops to prunes and then grapes, head to the **Healdsburg Museum** (221 Matheson St.; 707-431-3325; www.healdsburg museum.org), which has free admission and a collection of Pomo and Wappo Indian artifacts.

Healdsburg is surrounded by renowned Sonoma County wine appellations, including Alexander Valley, Chalk Hill, Dry Creek Valley, and Russian River Valley, and it is central to more than 100 wineries and tasting rooms. The choices can be overwhelming. Winery listings by appellation

Healdsburg Plaza
ROBERT HOLMES/ CALTOUR

The Camellia Inn
COURTESY OF THE CAMELLIA INN

and detailed information are available from the **Sonoma County Vintners** (707-522-5840, www.sonomawine.com).

For a tour of one of the oldest wineries, visit **Simi** (16275 Healdsburg Ave.; 800-746-4880; www .simiwinery.com), started in 1881 by two Italian brothers. The rustic-style tasting room has lots of history: look for the grove of redwood trees planted by the Simi family to celebrate the repeal of Prohibition in 1933.

In 2006, film director Francis Ford Coppola purchased the landmark Chateau Souverain winery just outside of town and in 2007 changed its name to **Rosso and Bianco** (300 Via Archimedes, Geyserville; 707-857-1400; www.rossobianco.com). Seven acres of vineyards surround the chateaulike winery. Coppola's movie memorabilia collection is scheduled to be relocated there from Coppola's Rubicon Estate Winery in Napa.

Near Rosso and Bianco, in the tiny town of Geyserville, is an example of a mom-and-pop operation: **Meeker Vineyards'** tasting room, located in a 100-year old bank building. The winery (21035 Geyserville Ave.; 707-431-2148; www.meekerwine.com), owned by a former Hollywood studio chief, is known for its hearty red varietals.

Back in Healdsburg, **Wine Country Bikes** (61 Front St.; 707-473-0610; www.winecountrybikes .com) rents bikes with racks for carrying wine bottles during self-guided tours of the Dry Creek and Alexander Valley wine areas. Most mornings the shop offers a guided bike tour up the west side of Dry Creek. The 20- to 25-mile jaunt, which includes a picnic lunch, follows quiet country roads over small rolling hills and stops at small wineries such as Bella and two or three others.

Summer temperatures in the area can soar to 100 degrees, and that's when locals head to **Healdsburg Veterans Memorial**

Beach (13839 Old Redwood Hwy.; 707-433-1625; www.sonoma -county.org), which has a large sandy patch and lawn area on the banks of the Russian River. But get there early on summer weekends for a parking spot; by midday, the lot is full.

What better place to take a cooking class than in the middle of an area sometimes referred to as America's Provence? Throughout the year, chefs and winemakers at the **Relish Culinary School** (707-431-9999, 877-759-1004; www.relishculinary.com) lead two- and three-hour programs on such seasonal topics as hunting and cooking winter mushrooms and preparing springtime brunches. Morning or multiday behind-the-scenes food tours of the plaza, cooking classes, and farmers' market tours are conducted regularly.

When you've had your fill of fine wine and food, head to the **Charles M. Schulz Museum** (2301 Hardies Ln.; 707-579-4452; www .schulzmuseum.org) in nearby Santa Rosa, a 15-minute drive south of Healdsburg. Opened in 2002, the museum is dedicated to the work of the late *Peanuts* cartoonist, who lived in Sonoma County for 40 years. Permanent exhibits include the studio where Schulz worked and a mural composed of 3,588 *Peanuts* comic strips, printed on ceramic tiles, that together create one larger image: Lucy holding a football as hapless Charlie Brown runs to kick it. Temporary exhibits often focus on the work of other cartoonists or offer a retrospective of an aspect of Schulz's art. Take a wander next door at the Redwood Empire Ice Arena, where Schulz lunched each day at the Warm Puppy Cafe, an eatery dedicated to everyone's favorite beagle.

■■■■ WHERE TO EAT

Few can spend time in Healdsburg without hitting **Downtown Bakery** (308A Center St.; 707-431-2719; www.downtownbakery.net) at least once for a pastry or homemade ice cream. Another bakery with delectable breads and picnic goodies is **Costeaux** (417 Healdsburg Ave.; 707-433-1913; www.costeaux.com). **Bovolo**, in the Plaza Farms food mall on the square (106 Matheson St.; 707-431-2962; www.plaza farms.com), is a laid-back cafe with terrific breakfasts. For lunch try the salami sandwiches; the meat is cured by the restaurant owner himself. Locals' dinner favorites include **Manzanita** (336 Healdsburg Ave.; 707-433-8111; www.manzanita336.com) for wood-fired pizzas and French-inspired dishes such as coq au vin paired with local vegetables.

Fun, casual **Willi's Seafood** (403 Healdsburg Ave.; 707-433-9191; www.willisseafood.net) serves small plates and fish dishes with a Latin flavor. **Dry Creek Kitchen** (317 Healdsburg Ave.; 707-431-0330; www.charliepalmer.com) never seems to disappoint as a sophisticated, fine-dining experience with inventive cuisine. Healdsburg is also home to one of the most highly acclaimed restaurants in the U.S., **Cyrus** (29 North St.; 707-433-3311; www.cyrusrestaurant.com), which garnered two stars from Michelin in 2007. Some plan their Healdsburg getaways around difficult-to-get reservations at Cyrus, so start calling weeks ahead of your trip to land a table.

▮▮▮▮ WHERE TO SLEEP

Among the many quaint inns in Healdsburg is the **Grape Leaf Inn** (539 Johnson St.; 707-433-8140; 866-433-8140; www.grapeleaf inn.com), a 106-year old, meticulously maintained Queen Anne Victorian in a leafy neighborhood. A highlight is the downstairs speakeasy, a plush wine bar where the innkeeper serves local wines and cheese each afternoon. Rooms are romantic: the Sangiovese Room has a king-sized, four-poster bed, a mahogany fireplace, and a two-person spa tub.

Another romantic spot is the six-room **Calderwood Inn** (25 W. Grant St.; 707-431-1110, 800-600-5444; www.calderwoodinn.com), which includes a wide front porch with white wicker furniture and a lush front garden that famed horticulturist Luther Burbank helped design. The Springkell, one of the most impressive rooms, is lined with Victorian-era wallpaper; it has a queen-size, four-poster bed and French doors leading to a private sitting area.

The **Camellia Inn** (211 North St.; 800-727-8182; www.camelliainn .com), a salmon-colored Italianate Victorian built in 1869 as a hospital, stands out because of its resortlike pool area. Rooms are plush and filled with antiques; some rooms have canopied beds. The most private is Tiffany, which has its own entrance and a large bathroom with whirlpool tub.

▮▮▮▮ LOCAL CONTACT

Healdsburg Chamber of Commerce and Visitors Bureau, visitors center at 217 Healdsburg Ave., 707-433-6935, www .healdsburg.org.

8 · THE RUSSIAN RIVER

Guerneville is about 75 miles north of San Francisco. Take US 101 north, exit on River Road, and head west.

The **Russian River** starts in the Mendocino County mountains north of Ukiah and flows south through Sonoma County, turning west at Healdsburg and rolling through several old resort towns before emptying out in the Pacific Ocean at Jenner.

Between Healdsburg and Jenner is an area that in the early 1900s became a popular vacation spot for San Franciscans escaping the summer fog. The villages here—Forestville, Guerneville, and Monte Rio—have kept their unpretentious, old-fashioned feel. The riverbanks are lined with small wooden cabins, some still not weatherproofed for winter living. This area of the river has undergone a lot of changes since its heyday as a family vacation spot from the 1920s to the 1950s. Hippies and bikers moved in during the 1960s, and gays settled here during the late 1970s and 1980s, sprucing up time-worn resorts.

Now there's a bit of gentrification, although not at the same levels as others part of the Sonoma wine country. You can still find King's Sport Tackle, an old bait shop on Main Street in Guerneville, the Russian River's largest town. And longtime residents have kept old traditions alive through the changes. At Guerneville's Holiday Parade of Lights on Main Street, you'll see the local Cub Scout troop marching along with a contingent of drag queens and a float from the local feed store.

The Russian River is known not only as a vacation spot but also for its wine, particularly pinot noirs, which grow well in the ocean-cooled Russian River valley. Many wineries are along lush, forested Westside Road, from Guerneville heading east. They include the valley's first winery, **Davis Bynum** (8075 Westside Rd.; 707-433-2611; www.davisbynum.com), which has a tasting room in a rustic barn; **Arista** (7015 Westside Rd.; 707-473-0606; www.aristawinery.com), surrounded by a Japanese garden; and historic **Hop Kiln** (6050 Westside Rd.; 707-433-6491; www.hopkilnwinery.com), which has a lovely picnic area.

Korbel Champagne Cellars (13250 River Rd.; 707-824-7000; www.korbel.com) is a favorite stopping point for visits to its old railroad station and antique-rose garden.

The focal point of any Russian River getaway, however, is the river, and the favorite way to explore it is by canoe. One mile north of Forestville, **Burke's** (8600 River Rd.; 707-887-1222; www.burkescanoetrips.com) rents canoes for 10-mile trips on gentle waters flowing past redwoods and pebbly beaches to Guerneville, where shuttle buses take paddlers back to their cars. The trip typically takes four or five hours, depending on how many stops are made. Pack a lunch in a cooler and bring swimsuits for dips in the cool river.

Just a block or two from the shops and restaurants of Guerneville, **Johnson's Beach** (16241 First St.; 707-869-2022; www.johnsonsbeach.com), on one of the widest stretches of the river, is a great place to hang out under an umbrella for the day. Canoes, kayaks, and paddleboats are for rent at this family-operated private beach, which is also the scene of two annual music events that draw top-name artists: the Russian River Blues Festival in June and Jazz on the River the weekend after Labor Day.

Two miles north of Guerneville is little-visited **Armstrong Redwoods State Reserve** (17020 Armstrong Woods Rd.; 707-869-2015; www.parks.ca.gov), an oasis of coastal redwoods that includes Colonel Armstrong, a tree over 1,400 years old, and the Parson Jones Tree, which, at 310 feet high, is longer than a football field. There are shady picnic spots and a self-guided nature trail that makes for a short, easy stroll.

Monte Rio, west of Guerneville on CA 116, is a quirky old vacation town that has not been touched by gentrification. The **Rio Theater** (707-865-0913; www.riotheater.com), housed in an old Quonset hut, is Sonoma County's last remaining rural single-screen movie theater, and it shows classics and current releases. The adjacent rocky beach is a lazy place to while away a summer afternoon watching the river flow by. For an overview of the local wine options, check out **Sophie's Cellars** in Monte Rio (20293 Hwy. 116; 707-865-1122; www.sophiescellars.com), which has a large selection of Russian River wines and suggestions for tasting rooms to visit.

From Monte Rio head west on CA 116 and take a right onto the tree-lined Cazadero Highway, which follows an old narrow-gauge railroad roadbed. Travel 6 miles to the redwood-surrounded hamlet of **Cazadero**, with its 100-year old general store. Across the street from the store, at the old lumber mill, ask if you can poke around Willys America, which restores old ambulances and other antique vehicles and has one of the country's largest collection of Willys. Stop at homey **Raymond's Bakery** (5400 Cazadero Hwy; 707-632-5335; www.raymonds-bakery.com) for a loaf of fresh bread, a slice of focaccia or pizza, or a cup of coffee to enjoy in the cafe or outside picnic tables.

Back on CA 116 head west and explore **Duncans Mills**, a collection of more than a dozen art shops and galleries. One weekend each July the powerful reverberations of old canons shake the town when one the largest Civil War reenactments in California (831-751-6978; www.civilwardays .net) takes place in a nearby meadow. Reenactors, costumed in period uniforms, set up elaborately re-created military camps and relive battles between Union and Confederate forces several times per day.

▪▪▪▪ WHERE TO EAT

The **Cape Fear Cafe** in Duncans Mills (25191 Main St.; 707-865-9246) dishes out Southern-style food three meals a day. Fried-oyster poor-boy sandwiches are a popular lunch special. The **Village Inn** in Monte Rio (20822 River Blvd.; 707-865-2304; www .villageinn-ca.com) has a lovely restaurant that is particularly appealing on a warm summer evening, when guests are served on the deck overlooking the river. For casual and fun, two old-time, family-run eateries are the **Russian River Pub** in Forestville (11829 River Rd.; 707-887-7932; www .russianriver.pub.com), with its big breakfasts and charbroiled burgers, and **Main Street Station** in Guerneville (16280 Main St.;

The Village Inn, Monte Rio, on the Russian River

The Raford Inn's Blueberry Room
COURTESY OF THE RAFORD INN

707-869-0501; www.main
station.com), serving pizza and
Italian food. Three miles south of
Forestville, in the village of Gra-
ton, **Willowood Cafe** (9020 Gra-
ton Rd.; 707-823-0233; www
.willowwoodgraton.com) attracts
locals with delicious, creative egg
dishes for breakfasts and hot
lunch sandwiches such as roasted
eggplant with feta, pesto, and
roast garlic mayonnaise. You'll
need advance reservations for two
acclaimed Forestville restaurants:
the **Farmhouse** (7871 River Rd.;
707-887-3300; www.farmhouse
inn.com) uses only local, organic
ingredients such as wild salmon
caught off the coast and produce
from the owner's farm; **Mosaic**
(6675 Front St.; 707-887-7503;
www.mosaiceats.com) generates
terrific reviews for its California-
global cuisine and a menu that
changes frequently to reflect
what's in season.

▪▪▪▪ WHERE TO SLEEP

The **Sonoma Orchid Inn** (12850
River Rd.; 707-887-1033, 888-
877-4466; www.sonomaorchidinn
.com) is a 1906 farmhouse with 10
rooms, including four cottages,
the prettiest of which is the
Madrone Suite with a private
patio. The Laurel Suite in the
main house, with a private sitting
area and porch, is a dream. The
orchid-loving owners invite

guests to bring their own orchids
to repot them in their green-
house. Breakfasts include eggs
fresh from the inn's own chicken
coop.

The **Village Inn** in Monte Rio
(see "Where to Eat") is so charming it looks like the set of a movie
–and indeed it was. The 1942 Bing
Crosby classic *Holiday Inn* was
partially filmed here. In 2001 the
inn was renovated by owners
Mark Belhumeur and Philip
Hampton, who provide gracious
hospitality. Among the primo
rooms are Room G in the main
building and Room 20 in the
annex; both have private decks
overlooking the river.

Perched above the river valley
on four acres, the **Raford Inn**
(10630 Wohler Rd.; 707-887-9573,
800-887-9503; www.rafordhouse
.com) is a bed-and-breakfast inn
in a beautiful 1880s home. A
large, porch invites guests to take
in vineyard views. The Angelica
Room is everyone's romantic
favorite: Large and private, it
features its own entrance, a front
porch, and a wood-burning fireplace.

▪▪▪▪ LOCAL CONTACT

**Russian River Chamber of Com-
merce**, visitors center at 16209
First St., Guerneville, 707-869-
9000, www.russianriver.com.

9 · CALISTOGA

Calistoga is 75 miles north of San Francisco and 18 miles north of Yountville (see chapter 5) on CA 29.

Back before spas were trendy, and long before wine put Napa on the map, **Calistoga** was the tourist spot of Napa Valley. Legend has it that the town's name came from a toast by promoter Sam Brannan; he intended to hail the town as "the Saratoga of California," but instead toasted "the Calistoga of Sarafornia." Early San Franciscans traveled to Calistoga for "cures," which consisted of soaking their creaky joints in dense, bubbling mud baths and sulfurous geothermal pools.

Today, the town is playing catch up to fancier spas in the rest of the country. Some of the older spas of Calistoga—which still have natural mineral water fed into their plumbing—are gussying themselves up to attract a new generation more interested in massages and blissful relaxation than doctor-ordered soaks.

Spa treatments are available at many establishments along the town's main boulevard, Lincoln Avenue, and its side streets. **Calistoga Spa Hot Springs** (1006 Washington St.; 707-942-6269; www.calistogaspa.com) is a longtime favorite of sun-starved San Franciscans, who come up for the day to dip into four outdoor mineral pools, each with water at different temperatures. Making it even more enjoyable is the opportunity for an evening swim: the pools are open until 9 PM. More glamorous is **Indian Springs** (1712 Lincoln Ave.; 707-942-4913; www.indianspringscalistoga .com), which dates back to 1861. It's a resort hotel, but day guests are welcome for spa treatments, which include access to the Olympic-size, warm-water mineral pool and the peaceful Buddha pond surrounded by palm trees. Both these spas pamper with the classic Calistoga "works": a mud bath followed by a mineral bath, steam bath, blanket wrap, and massage. Don't plan any activities—except for a long nap—for afterwards. A newer spa in town, upscale and geared to couples, **Lavender Hill** (1015 Foothill Blvd.; 707-942-4495; www.lavenderhillspa.com) offers massages and mud baths in little yellow cabins set in a garden. The mud used is not the thick gunk found elsewhere, but loosened up with lavender oils.

With less traffic than other parts of the valley, the Calistoga area lends itself particularly to bicycling, especially along the Silverado Trail with its wide shoulders The **Calistoga Bikeshop** (1318 Lincoln Ave.; 866-942-2453; www.calistogabikeshop.com) has created an innovative way to pedal the area and taste wine. For $79, the shop will set you up on a self-guided day tour with maps, wristbands for tastings at six wineries, and a bike with a picnic rack. The ride also includes a wine pick-up service: staffers collect your purchases from the wineries and have them waiting for you at the shop by 5 PM. Reservations for the ride are recommended. If you visit all six wineries (most make it to only four or five), it's an easy 16-mile bike ride.

One of the newest and most unusual wineries in all of Napa Valley is in Calistoga: **Castello di Amorosa** (4045 N. St. Helena Highway; 707-942-8200; www .castellodiamorosa.com), a labor of love for longtime winemaker Darryl Sattui. At the end of a long driveway, the 107-room replica of a medieval castle—with its moat and drawbridge, turrets and towers—looks like an apparition. Make reservations for an hour-long tour followed by wine tast-

ing. You'll see walls of hand-chiseled stone from a local quarry and old bricks from Europe, a dungeon with bone-chilling medieval torture devices, and underground rooms with wine barrels stored under beautiful vaulted ceilings.

Another impressive winery complex is **Clos Pegase** (1060 Dunaweal Ln.; 707-942-4981; www.clospegase.com), which includes wine caves, a cave theater that seats up to 350 people, museum-quality art, and a sculpture garden with works by Richard Serra and Henry Moore. The entire complex was designed by Michael Graves.

A nothing-fancy "boutique winery"—an example of how friendly and laid-back the valley's winemakers once were—is **Vincent Arroyo** (22361 Greenwood Ave.; 707-942-6995; www .vincentarroyo.com), known for its petit sirah, sold only at the winery.

For an in-depth look at the area's history, head to the **Sharpsteen Museum** (1311 Washington St.; 707-942-5911; www .sharpsteen-museum.org), just off Lincoln, where dioramas show Calistoga during its elegant, 1860s resort heyday. A room is devoted to the pioneer Sharpsteen family; the museum's founder, Ben Sharpsteen, was a

Indian Springs spa

Sculpture garden at Clos Pegase winery

Walt Disney animator and director, and one of his Academy Awards is on display.

Four miles south of Calistoga on CA 29 is **Bale Grist Mill State Historic Park** (3369 N. St. Helena Hwy.; 707-942-4575; www.parks .ca.gov). Its centerpiece is a mill, dating from 1846, that has a 36-foot wooden waterwheel. The park, open on weekends, has a store that sells cornmeal and flour freshly ground in the mill. From the store and the mill, walkers can follow the History Trail about 1½ miles north, past the mid-1800s Pioneer Cemetery, to **Bothe-Napa Valley State Park**. The park (same contact information as Bale Grist Mill) has a Native American plant garden, swimming pool, camping and picnic grounds. **Triple Creek Horse Outfit** (707-887-8700; www.triplecreekhorseoutfit.com) operates a stable in the park and offers hour-long guided rides on hillside redwood and Douglas fir forest trails.

▌▌▌▌ WHERE TO EAT

Although you can easily get in your car and drive to Napa Valley's destination restaurants in St. Helena and Yountville, after a day of spa treatments or wine tasting, you may not want to wander far. Calistoga has a good selection of restaurants, most of which are dress-down casual compared to the "down valley" counterparts. A favorite for its simple pub food and cozy atmosphere is **Calistoga Inn & Brewery** (1250 Lincoln Ave.; 707-942-4101; www.calistogainn.com); it's also popular for its patio and bar scene with live music most nights. **Wappo** (1226 Washington St.; 707-942-4712; www.wappo bar.com) serves food that is difficult to characterize; for example, its delicious chile relleno—filled with rice, currants, and cheese with a walnut pomegranate sauce—is anything but traditional. **Brannan's Grill** (1374 Lincoln Ave.; 707-942-2233; www

.brannansgrill.com) is another local favorite for its American and Italian food. The same owners recently opened **BarVino** (1457 Lincoln Ave.; 707-942-9900; www .mountviewhotel.com) at the Mount View Hotel and Spa (see "Where to Sleep"). With small plates of such items as crispy calamari with artichokes, plus a long menu of local wines by the glass, they're packing 'em in.

■■■■ WHERE TO SLEEP

Although not as tony as those of neighboring Napa Valley towns, Calistoga's inns and hotels have become more upscale the last five years. **Chanric Inn** (1805 Foothill Blvd.; 707-942-4535; www .chanricinn.com), a six-room bed-and-breakfast, resides in a lovely 1875 home that has been redecorated in a clean, modern style. A beautiful swimming pool with views of the Palisades mountain range makes it a top pick. Ask for rooms on the ground floor for more privacy. The breakfasts— three courses prepared by a

chef—are a highlight. The **Aurora Park Cottages** (1807 Foothill Blvd.; 877-942-7700; www.aurora park.com) next door features charming cabins, each with its own deck. The **Mount View Hotel** (1457 Lincoln Ave.; 707-942-6877; www.mountviewhotel.com) is a sumptuous, late Victorian-era charmer with fluffy feather beds and a spa and large outdoor pool. The **Cottage Grove Inn** (1711 Lincoln Ave.; 707-942-8400; www .cottagegrove.com) sits comfort- ably under 100-year old elm trees that create a cool, lush atmos- phere in this often-hot area. Its shabby-chic cottages feature wood-burning fireplaces and big bathrooms with two-person soak- ing tubs. Personable owner Donna Jackson ensures that guests have everything they need.

■■■■ LOCAL CONTACT

Calistoga Chamber of Com- merce, visitors center at 1506 Lin- coln Ave.; 707-942-6333; www .calistogachamber.com.

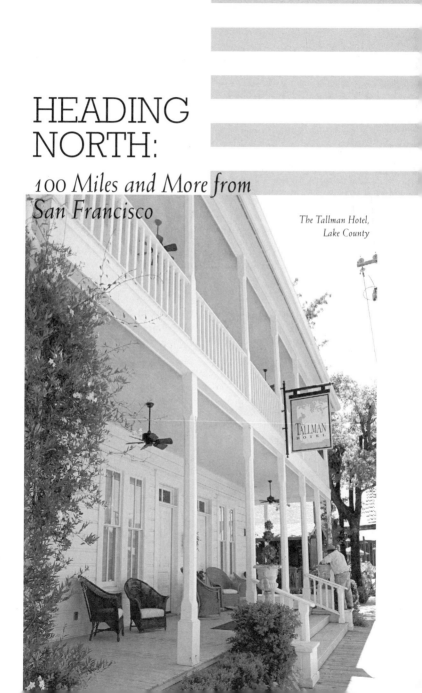

HEADING
NORTH:

*100 Miles and More from
San Francisco*

*The Tallman Hotel,
Lake County*

10 · BOONVILLE &
THE ANDERSON VALLEY

Boonville is 100 miles north of San Francisco. Take US 101 north to CA 128 west.

When you're driving to Mendocino, thinking about the crashing surf and the blue of the Pacific, you might take a rest stop along the twists and turns of CA 128 and find you've landed in a tiny town—perhaps Boonville, maybe Philo—in quiet, pastoral **Anderson Valley**. The hills are studded with oak trees, old wooden buildings, rows of vineyards backed by redwood groves, and the occasional flock of sheep grazing. Tractors slowly make their way on the highway shoulder. There isn't a stoplight for the valley's 25 miles. At that point, you may decide to return some day and spend more time here. Many people do.

The largest Anderson Valley town, **Boonville**, is four blocks long and has a population of less than a thousand. Turn-of-the-century buildings house a couple of shops, including **Bates and Maillard Farmhouse Mercantile** (14111 Hwy. 128), an upscale housewares boutique with jams and jellies from the nearby Philo Apple Farm. Pick up a copy of the *Anderson Valley Advertiser*, whose motto is "America's Last Newspaper" and rightly proclaims "you haven't read another newspaper like it because there isn't one" (quotations from Vladimir Lenin are interspersed with those of Joseph Pulitzer), and you'll get a feel for why the town residents make rich story material.

Anderson Valley always seems to have attracted eccentrics. Remote and isolated, the small population used its own language, Boontling, for years to confuse outsiders. Few speak it anymore, but words are occasionally thrown in local conversations to keep Boontling alive: you may get a "horn of zeese" (a cup of coffee) or take a "pike" (stroll) through town. If you're feeling poorly, someone may recommend a "shoveltooth," a medical doctor; the word derived from the local doctor who had a protruding tooth.

Once known for apple orchards and sheep ranches, Anderson Valley today is famous for pinot noir, gewürztraminer, and chardonnay. The oldest winery is **Husch** (4400 Hwy. 128; 800-554-8724; www.huschvineyards.com), which produces a grassy sauvignon blanc, samples of which are available in the rustic tasting room, a former grain storage shed. You can picnic on the deck or under the grape arbor. **Roederer Estate** (4501 Hwy. 128, Philo; 707-895-2288; www.roederer estate.net) is perhaps the best known of the wineries. The French-run operation—its parent created Cristal champagne—makes sparkling wines that have even beat French champagnes in international competitions. Tastings are in a lovely wooden building nestled on a hillside with vineyard views. For more winery information contact the **Anderson Valley Winegrowers** (707-895-9463; www.avwines .com).

Wine is not the only alcoholic beverage recognized in these parts. The **Anderson Valley Brewing Company** (17700 Hwy 253; 707-895-2337; www.avbc .com) is known for producing some of the state's best microbrews, all of them made with natural ingredients and no artificial preservatives. The brewery, which started in 1987, has a 30-barrel facility at the corner of CA 128 and CA 253, a mile from the center of Boonville. It includes a visitors center that serves beer and ale in 5-ounce glasses for sampling. Tours of the facility, which include copper kettles rescued from a defunct German brewery, are conducted each afternoon. The brewery uses local Boontling words in naming their brews, including their top-seller, Boont Amber Ale ("Boont" is Boonville). The staff may wish you "Bahl Hornin'"—good drinking.

May is a big month in Boonville. Not only are the hills a lush shade of green and covered with a riot of orange California poppies, but the Boonville Beer Festival also takes place in the fairgrounds. It's a time to sample national and locally made beer while listening and dancing to bands. It's also the month for the Pinot Noir Festival, which celebrates one of the area's prime varietals with winery open houses. May is also the start of the farmers' market, which runs on Saturday mornings through October in the Boonville Hotel parking lot. The market has more than fruit and vegetables: there are also breads, olive oils, and other local products.

Or stop at the **Philo Apple Farm**, 3 miles west of Philo (turn left at the Elk-Hendy Woods State Park Road, then turn left at the bridge and the farm) for some organic apple juice, cider, and jams and jellies. The owning families—three generations of the Schmitts and Bates—allow you to wander in their vegetable and flower garden. The farm also conducts weekend cooking courses so popular they are booked months in advance (see "Where to Sleep").

Eight miles northwest of Boonville is **Hendy Woods State Park** (Philo-Greenwood Rd., 707-895-3141; www.parks.ca.gov), where the Navarro River flows through virgin coastal redwood forests to the Pacific Ocean. Picnic sites line the riverbanks at Big Hendy Grove, one of the two majestic forests. Check at the ranger station for maps of the nature trails that wind through both Big and Little Hendy groves. One short, easy hike leads to the "hermit hut," a hollowed-out stump where Petrov, a Russian immigrant, lived for 18 years, largely by foraging for food in the woods.

People bring their own canoes and kayaks for a paddle down the **Navarro River** in late winter and early spring, but the river often gets too low by mid-summer for those activities. The waters are often too low even for swimming, although there's a reliable swimming spot underneath the Greenwood Bridge, just outside the park boundary. Swimming holes also can be found along CA 128 west, toward the coast in **Navarro River Redwoods State Park**, although this area can be chillier and foggier than Hendy Woods.

▮▮▮▮ WHERE TO EAT

In Boonville, the **Mosswood Market** (14111 Hwy. 128; 707-895-3635; www.mosswoodmarket.com) is a cafe that's turned into the town

Inside a cottage at the Boonville Hotel
COURTESY OF THE BOONVILLE HOTEL

A Boonville phone booth is labeled a "Bucky Walter," the term for telephone in Boontling, the local language.
ROBERT HOLMES/ CALTOUR

gathering place. Stop in for a quick breakfast or lunch of hot pressed sandwiches and a bowl of soup. **Boonville General Store** (Hwy. 128 across from the Boonville Hotel; 707-895-9477), another cafe, offers sandwiches for picnics. **Highpockety Ox** (14081 Hwy. 128; 707-895-2792; www.highpocketyox.com) serves pub food and a selection of 26 local wines and 30 beers, including beers from the Anderson Valley Brewing Company. You'll find live music on Saturday nights in the beer garden. Sophisticated fare using organic, local ingredients is the specialty at the **Boonville Hotel** (Hwy. 128 at Lambert Ln.; 707-895-2210; www.boonville hotel.com). A spring menu may start with warm asparagus with roasted peppers and shaved pecorino, follow with a Niman Ranch sirloin steak with potato-leek gratin, and end with rhubarb pie a la mode with a caramel swirl. In Philo, **Libby's** (8651 Hwy. 128; 707-895-2646) dishes out excellent Mexican fare; carnitas and daily specials such as petrale sole with salsa fresca draw regulars.

▪▪▪▪ WHERE TO SLEEP

The **Boonville Hotel** (see "Where to Eat"), built in 1870s, was recently renovated with contemporary furnishings, including locally made, "California shaker" style beds. Rooms facing the highway are spacious and have balconies, but street noise may bother some. In a separate building at the rear of the hotel are two quiet suites, the Bungalow and Studio, which have porches and outdoor sitting areas along a creek.

Ravenridge (707-894-7320; www.ravenridgecottages.com) in Yorkville, in the eastern end of Anderson Valley, features two stylishly decorated cottages set on hillsides under large oak trees. The Hillview is a one-bedroom with a living room and full kitchen; the Woodhaven a large one-room studio with kichenette and French doors opening to a deck. Each has wood-burning stove, satellite TV, and DVD players.

Philo Apple Farm (18501 Greenwood Rd., Philo; 707-895-2461; www.philoapplefarm.com) offers three simple, rustic cottages with colorful quilts, wood floors, and fresh flowers. They are reserved for cooking-class students most weekends; nonstudents can book midweek.

▪▪▪▪ LOCAL CONTACT

Anderson Valley Chamber of Commerce, 707-895-2379; www .andersonvalleychamber.com.

11 · LAKE COUNTY

Lake County is about 110 miles north of San Francisco. From Calistoga (see chapter 9), continue on CA 29 to Middletown.

Lake County has been called the "un-Napa," because although it is only a few miles as the crow flies from its tony neighbor, it's unpretentious and decidedly unchic. It's been a vacation spot for more than century for its central feature: Clear Lake, the largest freshwater lake in California. (Lake Tahoe is larger but lies partially in the state of Nevada.)

Clear Lake is a beautiful, sparkling body of water surrounded by pine- and oak-studded hills that are a burnt gold most of the year and turn emerald green in spring. The lake is cursed with hydrilla, a slimy weed that can make swimming unappealing. But don't let that put you off. The water is warm and a playground for people who love boating, waterskiing, fishing, and want to simply unwind. It also boasts some of the cleanest air in California, a fact you'll hear locals proudly proclaim.

You can drive around the lake's 100 miles of shoreline in a couple of hours and poke around its sleepy, small towns. Some are scruffy, with trailer parks and boarded-up storefronts, but some, like Middletown, Lakeport, Upper Lake, and Kelseyville, have a simple, small-town charm.

The county seat, **Lakeport**, on the west shore, has a population of only 5,100. Settled in the late 1850s, it retains a Victorian-era Main Street, which fronts the lake. A recommended first stop is Lakeport's visitors center (see "Local Contact"), perched on a hill, where there's a sweeping view of the lake. The **Lake County Historical Courthouse Museum** (255 N. Main St.; 707-263-4555; www.lakecounty.com) houses a display of 300 baskets from local Indian tribes.

Also on the west shore is quaint **Kelseyville**, which has a smattering of shops and hosts an annual Pear Festival the last Saturday of September. Festivities include art and antique tractor shows, a parade, and pear-packing competitions.

The town of **Lower Lake**, on the south shore, has some of the county's oldest buildings, including the area's first jail (16118 Main St.), a tiny stone structure that is among the smallest jails in the U.S. The **Lower Lake Historic Schoolhouse Museum** (16435 Morgan Valley Rd.; 707-995-3565; www.lakecounty.com) was built in 1877 and served as a school until 1935. Displays include period classrooms, a Victorian parlor, and mining artifacts. Just north of town is **Anderson Marsh State Historic Park** (Lower Lake; 707-994-0688; www.parks.ca.gov), offering nature trails great for bird-watching, a 19th century farmhouse (sometimes open for visitors; call ahead), and Pomo Indian archaeological sites.

There are many ways to take to the water at Clear Lake, including Jet Skis, pedal boats, motorboats, and wind surfboards. Rodman Slough, about a 10-minute drive from Lakeport, is a kayaking spot where a variety of birds (an osprey nest sits on top of a pole in the park's parking lot), fish, and plant life can be spotted. **Disney's Water Sports** in Lakeport (401 S. Main St.; 707-263-0969; www.disneyswatersports.com) rents kayaks and many kinds of boats, but it does not transport kayaks.

Clear Lake is known as an angler's paradise, especially for those fishing for bass, but catfish, trout, and other fish also are plentiful. The area has several boat and guide services, including two in Kelseyville: **Big George's** (707-279-9269; www.biggeorgesguide.com) and **Richard Pounds** (707-297-4739; www.bassfishinclearlake.com). A tackle and bait shop in Lakeport, called **Tackle It** (1050 Main St.; 707-262-1233; www.tackleit.biz), sells supplies.

Some plan Lake County vacations around the concert schedule at **Konocti Harbor** (8727 Soda Bay Rd.; Kelseyville; 707-279-4281; 800-660-LAKE; www.konoctiharbor.com), a 250-room, waterfront resort hotel. Its outdoor amphitheater hosts major artists (Bob Dylan played here in 2006), who perform under the stars. Check Konocti's schedule and book rooms well in advance when a big name is scheduled.

With the boom in Lake County wine growing (many Napa wineries actually buy their grapes in Lake County), more tasting rooms are opening. The atmosphere is more down-to-earth than in Napa, and tasting fees, if there are any, are about a third less. Wineries include **Steele**, owned by Jed Steele, the founding winemaker at Kendall Jackson. The tasting room (4350 Thomas Dr. at Hwy. 29, Kelseyville; 707-279-9475; www.steelewines.com) is a pleasant stop, especially for the Saturday morning farmers' market, which runs from Memorial Day through October. On the east shore, **Ceago Del Lago Winery** (5115 E. Hwy. 20, Nice; 707-274-1462; www.ceago.com) is a lavish Mediterranean-style winery that looks a bit out of place with its perfectly landscaped gardens and elegant tasting room (think Napa). Ceago is owned by Jim Fetzer, whose family owned the winery of the same name in Mendocino County and started Ceago after selling Fetzer.

East of Middletown, tucked in a valley, is **Langtry Estate** (formerly Guenoc and now named after the Victorian actress Lillie Langtry, who planted grapes here 100 years ago). The winery is known for its petit sirah and crisp sauvignon blancs. The tasting room (21000 Butts Canyon Rd.; 707-987-9127; www.langtry estate.com) has lovely picnic grounds.

Walnut and pear orchards are giving way to grape growing, but there's plenty of traditional agriculture left. Lake County remains the second largest pear producer in the U.S. Produce stands include **Hanson Ranch** (3360 Merritt Rd., Kelseyville; 707-279-4761), which has local pears and walnuts, and **Sutton Family Farm** (2218 Hendricks Rd., Lakeport; 707-263-6277), which sells lettuce, spinach, and other vegetables.

▪▪▪▪ WHERE TO EAT

The town of Upper Lake was settled in the 1840s and looks like an Old West movie set. The **Blue Wing Saloon** (9520 Main St.; 707-275-2233; www.bluewingsaloon .com), adjacent to the Tallman Hotel (see "Where to Sleep"), seems like it's been there as long as the town but was actually constructed in 2004 as a replica of an old tavern. The restaurant specializes in "California comfort food," including mashed potatoes, braised short ribs, and portobello-mushroom ravioli. There's live blues music on Monday nights.

People drive for miles to have a cup of joe at **Studebaker's Coffee House** (3990 Main St., Kelseyville; 707-279-8871; www.studebakers coffee.com), which also serves sandwiches, Italian gelato, and pastries. Down the block, **Saw Shop Gallery Bistro** (3825 Main St., Kelseyville; 707-278-0129; www.sawshopbistro.com) is a gourmet, dinner-only restaurant offering an eclectic menu in an art-gallery setting. A nice touch is a corkage fee of only $10, half of which is donated to Habitat for Humanity.

▪▪▪▪ WHERE TO SLEEP

Bernard and Lynne Butcher bought the run-down 1870 building at the end of Upper Lake's

Ceago Del Lago Winery

Featherbed Railroad Inn

main drag in 2003 and spent four years painstakingly transforming it into the **Tallman Hotel** (9550 Main St.; 707-275-2244, 866-708-5253; www.tallmanhotel.com). Their attention to detail shows in the fine furniture, linens, and antique plumbing, which includes half-circular shower fixtures with jets that in Victorian times allowed women to shower without getting their hair wet. The historic rooms in the main building have French doors opening onto wide verandas. Four rooms in a new building out back have patios with Japanese soaking tubs. A pretty swimming pool area adds to a resortlike vibe.

In Lakeport, the five-room **Arbor House** (150 Clearlake Ave.; 707-263-6444; www.arborhouse bnb.com), run by former Bay Area residents Karen and Sam Karnatz, has a rose garden and outdoor whirlpool tub. Rooms in the 1905 Victorian have their own entrances and porches. The Courtyard Suite in the back has the most privacy.

On the eastern side of the lake is **the Bungalow** (10195 E. Hwy. 20, Clearlake Oaks; 707-998-0399; www.thebungalow.com). Formerly a 1930s restaurant built in the Arts and Crafts style, it was gutted in 2004, except for its original dance floor and vaulted ceiling. Now it is a three-room bed-and-breakfast, and the warm hospitality of the former schoolteacher owners make it a good choice for those looking for a homey atmosphere. Kayaks and canoes are available for guests, who can also use the lakeside outdoor kitchen and barbecues. The Rose Suite, with its corner stained glass window, is especially nice. The Bungalow is open only from mid-May through October.

Featherbed Railroad Company (2870 Lakeshore Blvd.; 707-274-8378, 800-966-6322; www .featherbedrailroad.com) is a bed-and-breakfast inn for train lovers or anyone looking for a quirky place to spend the night. Guests stay in real cabooses (retired from Sante Fe and other railroads) that the owners saved from destruction. Each was renovated to have its own bathroom, featherbeds, and frilly Victorian-period furnishings. Many have two-person whirlpool tubs. Tandem bicycles are available for guest use, a dock is steps away, and a swimming pool provides cool relief.

▮▮▮▮ LOCAL CONTACT

Lakeport Chamber of Commerce, visitors center at 875 Lakeport Blvd., 707-263-5092, 800-525-3743; www.lakeportchamber.com. **Lake County Visitors Information Center**, visitors center at 6110 E. Hwy. 20, Lucerne, 707-274-5652, 800-525-3743, www.lakecounty.com.

12 • SONOMA'S NORTH COAST

Gualala is 120 miles north of San Francisco. Follow directions for Bodega Bay (chapter 6) and continue north on CA 1.

CA 1 snakes through the town of Jenner north of the Russian River Bridge, twisting through horseshoe turns and along steep cliffs as the ocean crashes below. This is Sonoma County's northern coast, a refuge where you can spend hours in solitude on remote beaches, any signs of civilization miles away.

Twelve miles north of Jenner you'll find isolated, windswept **Fort Ross**, founded in 1812 by Russian fur traders, who made it the easternmost outpost of tsarist Russia for 30 years. Today the fort is a state historic park (707-847-3286; www.parks.ca.gov). Its visitors center traces the history of the local tribes and the Russians' fur-trapping efforts from a time when seal and sea otter pelts could generate fortunes. Several buildings in the old fort are open for wandering, including the kitchen, the stockade, an officer's home, and a cupola-topped Russian Orthodox chapel from 1824. On weekends costumed docents evoke the atmosphere of the period. When you've seen the fort, follow the gravel road from the main gate to Fort Ross Cove, the site of an old shipyard, where driftwood and rocks are shaped by the ocean waves.

Salt Point State Park (707-847-3221; www.parks.ca.gov), 9 miles north of Fort Ross, has a particularly beautiful stretch of coastline with thick layers of exposed sandstone rock that look like walls of ancient Mayan temples. The windswept beaches seem made for long walks, beachcombing, and tide-pool exploration. One of the easiest walks is along the bluffs on the Salt Point Trail, a 2.4-mile round-trip hike from the Salt Point day-use area to Stump Beach, one of the few sandy beaches in the area.

At Gualala you reach the "banana belt," a 5-mile strip where you can peel off the layered clothing and enjoy more blue skies than typically found on other stretches of the fog-bound Sonoma or Mendocino coasts. The Gualala River flows through **Gualala Point Regional Park** (42401 Hwy. 1; 707-785-2377; www.sonoma-county.org) visitors center, 1 mile south of Gualala, making it a popular spot for picnickers.

Mother Nature contributes to fun on the river. Some time between mid-May and early July ocean waves build up the sand at the mouth of the Gualala, creating a sand bar that becomes a natural dam. The water backs up for several miles, turning the river into a long lake, which winds through redwood forests to the ocean, passing salt marshes and sandy beaches on the way. The water temperature warms up to 70 degrees, making the river much better for swimming than the chilly Pacific. The water is also ideal for leisurely kayaking; **Adventure Rents** (39175 S. Hwy. 1, behind Cantamore Center; 707-884-4386; www.adventurerents .com) provides equipment.

The town of **Gualala** doesn't have a lot of charm, but the still-isolated lumber town—which didn't get electricity until 1952—is surrounded by gorgeous beaches and redwood forests. The town's name is a Pomo Indian word meaning "where the water flows down" and is pronounced *wa-LA-la*. But even some natives pronounce it *goo-ah-LA-la* and will insist they are right. Stop for a drink at the Gualala Hotel, which oozes old-lumber-town character. The former stagecoach

stop was built in 1903 and has a lively pool hall in the back, where flannel-clad locals mix with artist types quaffing local ales such as Mendocino's Red Tale and Blue Heron. Nearby is a little culture, the **Gualala Arts Center** (46501 Gualala Rd.; 707-884-1138; www .gualalaarts.org), where the many artists who have settled in the area display their work.

▪▪▪▪ WHERE TO EAT

The restaurant at **Sea Ranch Lodge** (60 Sea Walk Dr.; 707-785-2371; 800-732-7262; www.sea ranchlodge.com) has large, floor-to-ceiling windows overlooking the bluffs and is a prime spot for watching the sunset. The menu's delicious selections include California cuisine made from mostly local ingredients.

At **Twofish Baking Company** (35590 Verdant View, the Sea Ranch; 707-785-2443; www.two fishbakery.com) people line up at 7 AM for sticky buns. The small cafe serves breakfast and lunch.

In Gualala, **St. Orres** (36601 Hwy. 1; 707-884-3303; www.saint orres.com) specializes in fresh local fish and game, such as pheasant, venison, and boar. There always is also a vegetarian selection or two, such as wild mushroom ravioli. **Pangaea** (39165 Hwy. 1; 707-884-9669; www.pangaeacafe.com)

describes its food as "lusty, zaftig, and soulful." All ingredients are grown or produced within a 30-mile radius of Gualala. The wild salmon is caught nearby, and breads are baked in the restaurant's own wood-fired oven.

▪▪▪▪ WHERE TO SLEEP

Sea Ranch Lodge (see contact information in "Where to Eat") may seem vaguely familiar if you've spent much time in Northern California. Built as an ecologically sensitive destination in the 1970s, years before the environmental movement took shape, the Sea Ranch's architecture of weathered natural wood and large windows echo up and down the coast here. The buildings, surrounded by native gardens, blend into the surrounding landscape. There are still no TVs and little nightlife, save the cozy bar in the main lodge. Most vacationers come here for weekly house rentals, but you can also stay on a nightly basis in the lodge. Room 12, with its huge windows and ocean views, is an example of the striking minimalist décor that brings the outside in.

You can't miss **St. Orres** (see contact information in "Where to Eat") and its onion domes that reflect the Russian heritage of the area. Eight small rooms in the

main building share baths. The highlights are the cottages spread across the forested grounds. The Treehouse, with a soaking tub, sitting area, fireplace, and French doors to a deck with partial ocean view, is a favorite. Across the St. Orres Creek

St. Orres hotel and restaurant, Gualala

The chapel at Fort Ross State Historic Park
ROBERT HOLMES/CALTOUR

are eight more cottages that share exclusive use of a hot tub, sauna, and sun deck.

The **North Coast Country Inn** (34591 Hwy. I; 707-884-4537; www.northcoastcountryinn.com), tucked away on a curve of CA I, immediately enchants with a large bell to call the innkeeper to greet guests at the front door. Rooms are pleasantly country, not too frilly, and there is a lush garden with a redwood gazebo.

Chocolates and a bottle of wine await guests. The Aquataine and Quilt rooms, with their colorful wainscoting, are warm and cozy but have the rugged feel of the north coast. The place was, in fact, one part of a sheep ranch.

▌▌▌▌ LOCAL CONTACT

Redwood Coast Chamber of Commerce, visitors center at 39150 S. Highway I; 707-884-1080; www.redwoodcoastchamber.com.

13 · THE MENDOCINO COAST

Mendocino is 155 miles north of San Francisco. From Boonville (see chapter 10), continue on CA 128 west, which merges onto CA 1, and head north.

Mendocino County's rugged coast, lined with rocky coves and crashing waves, makes an idyllic, romantic-getaway destination today, but when it was first settled it was anything but that. The coastal conditions were treacherous for Gold Rush—era schooners that sailed the rough waters. Shipwrecks led, indirectly, to the founding of the town of **Mendocino**.

Today a cluster of 19th-century wooden houses, surrounded by grassy, windswept ocean bluffs on three sides, Mendocino boomed with the Gold Rush. The population of San Francisco swelled from 6,000 to 20,000 in just a few months in 1849, making lumber scarce and very valuable. News of the shipwreck of a cargo-laden ship bound for China drew Jerome Ford north from San Francisco. Instead of sunken treasure, Ford discovered virgin redwood forests and found a site for Mendocino's first lumber mill. The north-coast lumber industry was born.

Mendocino thrived and then boomed again after the 1906 San Francisco earthquake, when the forests became key to rebuilding the city. Schooners that maneuvered in and out of the coves here carried up to a million board feet of lumber down the coast.

Ford built a home on the town bluffs when he married Martha Hayes, a Connecticut woman who arrived in 1854 to find she was one of only three women in town. The couple lived in the house until 1872, raising six children. Now the house is the **Ford House Museum** (735 Main St.; 707-937-5397; www.mendocino.com), where well-schooled volunteers describe local history using a scale model of the town in 1890.

From the Ford museum, take in the cool, salty air by walking along Main Street, looking in at the 1868 Presbyterian church built of redwood (its steeple is a town landmark) and an array of art galleries and jewelry shops. Many of the early Mendocino settlers were from New England, and their influence is reflected in the architecture. You can see why the town shows up in movies and on TV, often as a stand-in for a New

England village. Perhaps its best-known role was as the setting for TV's *Murder, She Wrote*, starring Angela Lansbury.

Adding to Mendocino's charm are the more than a dozen water towers that poke up above the roofs. The town still does not have a public water system, so many towers are in use; others have been converted to dwellings or shops. Check out the tower at 611 Albion Street, which houses the gallery, studio, and home of painter Suzi Long. Another rises in the garden at the **Kelley House Museum** (45007 Albion St.; 707-937-5791; www.mendocinohistory.org), a Victorian home containing historical photos of Mendocino's logging and shipping industries.

On three sides of town, trails curl alongside the sandstone cliffs that make up **Mendocino Headlands State Park** (707-937-5804; www.parks.ca.gov). The park, created in 1974 when rumors of a planned oceanside development stirred an anti-growth movement, is a treasure of grassy meadows and bluff paths. Several trail entrances radiate from Main Street, including one at the junction of Main and Heeser, where you can continue east for a 3-mile round-trip hike. Paths from here also lead down bluffs to Big River Beach,

which is lovely for beachcombing. Winds that commonly blow along the coast are less fierce on this protected beach, making it a good picnic site. To reach the trails along the windswept bluffs west and north of Mendocino, follow Little Lake Street west; after a short walk or five-minute drive, you'll reach the parking lot of an overlook, and the trails start there.

Big River, the estuary that was integral for transporting giant redwoods to the mill on the Mendocino headlands in the late 1800s, is easily explored by kayak or canoe. **Catch a Canoe** (Hwy. 1 at Comptche Ukiah Rd.; 707-937-0273; www.catchacanoe.com) offers rentals on the river's shore for easy paddle trips to canyons and swimming holes, where you may see river otters and a variety of birds. Call ahead, so that trips can be synchronized with tidal conditions.

In 1908, to protect schooners carrying lumber from Mendocino forests, the U.S. government erected the **Point Cabrillo Light Station** 2 miles north of Mendocino. The facility (707-937-6120; www.pointcabrillo.org) was home to three families, who operated the kerosene lamps. The station's light shone through a third-order Fresnel lens that had hundreds of prisms and was turned by a pendulum-style clockwork. Since its restoration, the lens has been back in operation, its light is visible up to 15 miles from shore. The visitors center tells about wrecks of opium-running ships and of the *Frolic*, the China-bound ship that changed the coast forever when it brought early settler Ford and others north. It also describes the hard work of the keepers who kept the lights burning, the lens cleaned, and the compressors powered.

Nearby is beautiful **Russian Gulch State Park** (707-937-5804; www.parks.ca.gov), known for its forested canyon and the Devil's Punch Bowl, a large blowhole in the headlands where the ocean churns and spouts like a geyser during storms or high tides. Trails here line the headlands.

Fort Bragg, 9 miles north of Mendocino, was a working-class lumber town but is depending more and more on tourism now that the main mill has closed. Downtown, a Sears store and

JCPenney catalog shop reside alongside high-end gift shops, newcomers on the scene. There's evidence of a thriving community of artists and back-to-nature types; you may spot someone wearing a "Get the Glow" t-shirt from **Living Light** (301-B North Main St.; 707-964-2420; www.raw foodchef.com), a vegan, raw-food culinary school where the chef prepares gazpacho, salads, and even a vegan, raw-food lasagna for takeaway.

Fort Bragg is the home of the **Mendocino Coast Botanical Gardens** (18220 Hwy. 1; 707-964-4352, www.gardenbythesea.org), a 47-acre explosion of color. Spring is rhododendron season, and late summer and fall bring heritage roses, fuchsias, hydrangeas, and dahlias. A garden store features a nursery with plants for sale.

At Glass Beach, a short walk from downtown, at the end of Elm Street, tide pools are full of starfish, anemones, and sea urchins, and the residue of an old dump site has been pounded and

The Ford House Museum in Mendocino Headlands State Park

The historic Mendocino Hotel

rounded by the ocean to create a kaleidoscope of colorful, glasslike stones. The beach is part of **MacKerricher State Park** (707-964-9112; www.parks.ca.gov), an expanse of beaches, tide pools, a freshwater lake, and coastal hiking trails 3 miles north of Fort Bragg. The park was once part of Union Lumber Company's swath of land holdings here. One easy, ¾-mile-long walk starts from the parking lot and circles Lake Cleone, following a boardwalk over a marsh, where you may see herons and egrets. Unusual for a state park, admission is free.

■■■■ WHERE TO EAT

It may be difficult to have a bad meal in Mendocino. It certainly will be difficult if your taste runs to fast-food joints: there aren't any. But you can have a juicy, grass-fed beef burger at **Moosses's** (Kasten at Albion; 707-937-4323; www.themoosse.com). Mendocino is the home one of the best-known restaurants in the region, **Cafe Beaujolais** (961 Ukiah St.; 707-937-5614; www.cafebeaujolais.com). Original owner and cookbook author Margaret Fox no longer owns the place, but it's still a top spot in town for its French-inspired food. Or, get there at 11 AM to buy a delicious loaf of bread straight from the wood-fired ovens. To round out your picnic supplies, mosey over to **Harvest** at Mendosa's grocery store (10501 Lansing St.; 707-937-5879; www.harvestmarket.com). **Mendocino Bakery** (10438 Lansing St.; 707-937-0836) is a breakfast and lunch cafe, serving sandwiches, salads, and coffee from beans roasted at the local Thanksgiving Coffee Company. For a scoop of locally made Cowlick's ice cream, don't miss **Frankie's** (10481 Lansing; 707-937-2436), an old-fashioned shop.

In Fort Bragg, **Mendo Bistro** (Main and Redwood streets; 707-964-4974; www.mendobistro.com) is renowned for its crab cakes and use of local, seasonal ingredients. The **Headlands Coffeehouse** (120 E. Laurel St.; 707-964-1987; www.headlandscoffeehouse.com) is the place where residents go for their caffeine fix, casual eats, and live evening music.

■■■■ WHERE TO SLEEP

Nothing may compare to a stay at a lighthouse for recreating the lives of the early coastal settlers. The **Lighthouse Inn** at Point Cabrillo (707-937-6124, 866-937-6124; www.mendocinolighthouse.pointcabrillo.org), a former light keeper's family home, was meticulously restored and opened in 2006 by a nonprofit group. The red-roofed house has period furniture in its four guest rooms. Guest-only bonuses are the five-course breakfasts and guided tours of the light station by night.

Brewery Gulch Inn (9401 Hwy. 1; 707-937-4752, 800-578-4454; www.brewerygulchinn.com) is the brainchild of Arky Ciancutti, a former emergency-room doctor. He salvaged local redwood, including 150-year old submerged logs from the nearby Big River, to build his hotel. The Raven room, with its ocean views and balcony, is a romantic favorite. The cooked-to-order breakfasts draw raves, and evening hors d'oeuvres are so generous that some guests end up canceling dinner reservations and cocooning for the evening.

A sweetly purring cat greets guests at the registration counter of the **Little River Inn** (7901 Hwy. 1; 707-937-5942, 888-466-5683; www.littleriverinn.com), a Victorian landmark owned by the same family for generations. Rooms in the new annex are swanky, but those in the old wing, such as number 115, with its fireplace and large balcony, are still charming

and a good value. In an area not known for its nightlife, Little River's bar is a fun local hangout and sometimes has live music.

If you'd like to be in town and bed-and-breakfasts aren't your style, the **Mendocino Hotel** (45080 Main St.; 707-937-0511, 800-548-0513; www.mendocino hotel.com) is a good choice. Sit at the lobby's fireplace—where guests have relaxed since the hotel opened in 1878—and look out at the crashing waves. Rooms with private baths in the old building include number 206, which has good views off a small balcony, and number 218, which is small but has a good-sized balcony. Rooms in the 1980s annex are larger and more luxurious. As befits a hotel with such a long history, rumor has it that there's a resident ghost: a Victorian woman who haunts the dining room and lobby.

▪▪▪▪ LOCAL CONTACT

Mendocino Coast Chamber of Commerce, 707-961-6300, www .mendocino.winecountry.com. **Mendocino County Alliance**, 707-462-7417, www.gomendo .com.

HEADING EAST:

Within 100 Miles of San Francisco

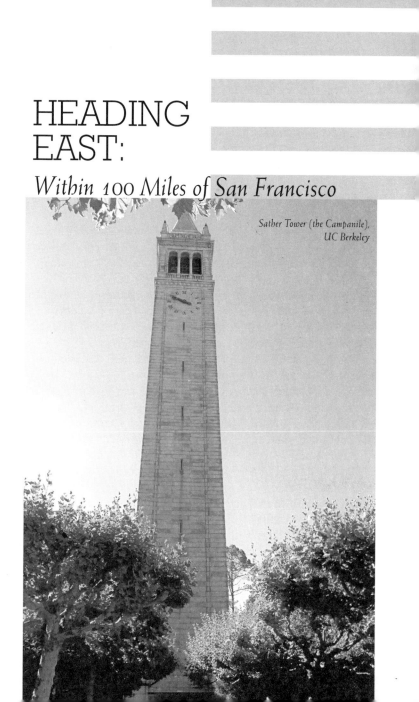

Sather Tower (the Campanile), UC Berkeley

14 • BERKELEY & OAKLAND

Berkeley and Oakland are just east of San Francisco, on I-80 across the San Francisco–Oakland Bay Bridge. Continue on I-80 and take the University Avenue exit for the University of California (UC) Berkeley.

More than just a college town of students and professors, **Berkeley** is a mix of political idealists, eco-warriors, organic entrepreneurs, New Age seekers, tie-dyed old hippies and younger wannabes, not to mention just plain folks.

With its history of the Free Speech Movement, People's Park, and antiwar protests, as well as its vibe of academic prestige and coffeehouse intellectualism, Berkeley's streets attract the sympathetic, the curious, and fire-and-brimstone sidewalk preachers. Thousands visit the campus and walk along **Telegraph Avenue**, the slightly scruffy but bustling street lined with old record stores, student pubs, cafes, bookstores, head shops, and used clothing outlets.

Free, 90-minute tours of the university campus are conducted daily. During the week these start at the visitors center at 101 University Hall at the corner of University Avenue and Oxford Street; on weekends they begin at the **Campanile bell tower** (510-642-5215; www.berkeley.edu). The tours take in several campus buildings, including the majestic main library (UC Berkeley has libraries for nearly every field of research, and many libraries have unique collections) and Valley Life Sciences Building, which houses the mounted skeleton of a *Tyrannosaurus rex*. Guides discuss university history, including the turbulent 1960s.

The Campanile, also known as Sather Tower, is a Bay Area landmark that dates from 1914. An elevator carries visitors up the 307-foot spire for a terrific view of the campus and points beyond. Just above the tower's observation platform, a carillon of 61 bells—the smallest 19 pounds, the heaviest 5 tons—plays at intervals through the day. Some may want to avoid visiting during that time; others may find it a literal and figurative blast being up there when the bells go off. Elevator operators usually warn visitors of bell tolls in advance.

Berkeley is a perfect place to sample the Bay Area's multiethnic food offerings, especially on

Shattuck Avenue between Cedar and Vine streets, a stretch known as the **Gourmet Ghetto**. It was here that Alice Waters opened Chez Panisse in 1971 and launched a way of eating—focusing on organic, local, in-season food—that has become a cultural movement (See "Where to Eat"). The Thursday farmers' market (3 to 7 PM) on Shattuck is a wonder of organically grown produce. A block east of Shattuck at the corner of Walnut and Vine is the original Peet's Coffee, a pioneer in dark-roasted coffee when it opened in 1966 (five years before Starbucks in Seattle).

For a pleasant and pretty stroll, walk north on Shattuck to **Live Oak Park** through a leafy neighborhood of Craftsman homes, and then stop for a picnic or just relax under the trees. If you'd like a longer walk, continue on a mile or so to **Indian Rock**, a small park surrounding an outcropping used for training by mountaineers. On the top of the rock, up steps carved into the stone, is a bay panorama that includes the Golden Gate Bridge.

Two places to see the making of food and drink are in West Berkeley. In a lovely tasting room of traditional Japanese architecture, **Takara Sake** (708 Addison St.; 510-540-8250; www.takara sake.com) offers free tastings of plum wines and sake made from pure Sierra Nevada snowmelt. A sake museum shows the drink's history in the United States. About a mile south is **Scharffen Berger** (914 Heinz Ave.; 510-981-4066;www.scharffenberger.com), a Willy Wonka fantasy come to life in a thick-walled, old brick munitions factory (yes, in pacifist Berkeley). Tours tell of chocolate history and the growth of premium brands. A gift shop sells chocolate-themed souvenirs, and an adjacent cafe serves, not surprisingly, delectable brownies.

Tilden Regional Park (510-843-2137; www.ebparks.org) is Berkeley's 2,000-acre backyard—a place to ride an old steam train, gather friends and family for picnics in forested meadows, swim in a lake, and stroll through canyons and gardens. Take Centennial Drive from the UC Berkeley campus past the Lawrence Hall of Science and enter the park at South Park Drive, following signs to the botanical garden. Founded in 1940, the 10-acre garden is dedicated to the preservation of California native plants; it is divided into 10 sections, each representing a distinctive natural area of the state, from desert to redwood forests. Various plants bloom from mid-December through October.

Continue on South Park Drive

past meadows and forested picnic areas to Grizzly Peak Boulevard and take a left, following the sign to the **Redwood Valley Railway**. This miniature railroad has been in operation since 1952. Its steam locomotives take delighted children and adults on 12-minute rides through the canyon.

After the railway, take a right on Grizzly Peak Boulevard to get back to Berkeley, and on the way enjoy some of the best views of the Bay Area anywhere. Several vista points on the steep, curvy road are particularly awesome spots from which to watch sunsets.

Berkeley's bigger neighbor, **Oakland**, is a city that deserves as much respect. It's a culturally diverse place with a historic downtown, beautiful neighborhoods, an excellent museum, and lovely **Lake Merritt**, whose 3-mile path attracts hundreds for jogging and walking and where a string of hundreds of lights twinkle at night. The boating center (568 Bellevue Ave.; 510-238-2196; www.oaklandnet.com) rents canoes, pedal boats, sailboats, or kayaks for exploring on this natural pond, the largest urban saltwater lake in the country.

The **Oakland Museum of California** (1000 Oak St. at 10th; 510-238-2200;www.museumca.org) is a vast storehouse of California historical treasures, with 6,000 artifacts, including a large collection of Native American baskets and an antique San Francisco fire engine that was put to much service in the 1906 earthquake.

Jack London Square on the Oakland Estuary is where the city was founded in 1852. Today, the square is full of shops, restaurants, and clubs, including one of the Bay Area's best for jazz; **Yoshi's** (510 Embarcadero West;

The Claremont Resort, Oakland
COURTESY OF THE CLAREMONT RESORT

510-238-9200; www.yoshis.com) serves excellent Japanese food and hosts top jazz musicians. The square still shows links to a literary past. At **Heinold's First and Last Chance Saloon** (48 Webster St.), built in 1880 from the timbers of a whaling ship, Jack London spent many an hour, starting at age 10 when he sold newspapers and listened to sailor stories. Step in carefully: The floors are uneven, and that's before you've had a drink. It's one of the few places listed on the National Register of Historic Places where you can sip a beer.

▪▪▪▪ WHERE TO EAT

In the middle of Berkeley's Gourmet Ghetto is stylish **Cesar** (1515 Shattuck Ave.; 888-281-7865; www.barcesar.com), the brainchild of Chez Panisse alumni. The food is small plates of Spanish-style tapas. There's a second, larger location at 4039 Piedmont Avenue in Oakland. Also on Shattuck is the **Cheeseboard Collective** (1504 Shattuck Ave.; 510-549-3183; www.cheeseboardcollective .coop), offering a dazzling array of international and domestic cheese and crusty breads. Two doors down at 1512 Shattuck is the worker-owned company's pizzeria, its mouth-watering pies sold by the slice.

Indulge in a sweet at a pretty little "cupcakery" called **Love at First Bite** (1510-G Walnut St.; 510-848-5727; www.loveatfirstbite bakery.com), which sells such innovative, pastel-colored creations as a lemon pistachio or bunny love (carrot) cupcakes. **Chez Panisse** (1517 Shattuck Ave.; 510-548-5525; www.chezpanisse .com) is the star on Shattuck. Both the cafe, open for lunch and dinner, and the restaurant, which has two seatings for dinner each night and one fixed-price menu, require reservations at least one calendar month ahead. Fine food is abundant elsewhere in Berkeley, including the hip Fourth Street retail corridor. It's the home of Japanese-California fusion specialist **O Chame** (1830 Fourth St.; 510-841-8783; www .themenupage.com) and **Eccolo** (1820 Fourth St.; 510-644-0444; www.eccolo.com), an Italian restaurant that gives a nod to American tastes with grilled hamburgers. Nearby, there's hole-in-the-wall **Vik's Chaat Corner** (724 Allston Way; 510-644-4412;www.vikdistributors .com), which lures customers with earthy Indian food. Oakland's Piedmont Avenue is another area chockablock with fine eateries, including the elegant **Bay Wolf** (3853 Piedmont Ave.; 510-655-6004; www.baywolf .com) with its imaginative

Mediterranean-California cuisine. More casual but no less popular is **Dopo** (4293 Piedmont Ave.; 510-652-3676), an Italian restaurant that attracts a following for its pizzas and pasta. In the charming, European-style Rockridge neighborhood, **A Cote** (5478 College Ave.; 510-655-6469; www.acoterestaurant.com) is known for small dishes normally served *a la cote*, "on the side," particularly fries and mussels in Pernod sauce.

▪▪▪▪ WHERE TO SLEEP

The **Claremont Resort** (41 Tunnel Rd.; 510-843-3000, 800-551-7266; www.claremontresort.com) is the most distinctive of Berkeley-Oakland's hotels; its white, castlelike turrets and towers in the Oakland Hills are landmarks. The hotel's recent renovation added a swanky day spa. For a special occasion, splurge on a room with views. Check online for packages for good deals. Try the Claremont's Paragon lounge for cocktails at sunset, when you'll see awesome views of San Francisco and the bay.

With sailboats moored alongside and compelling views of San Francisco across the bay, the **Waterfront Plaza Hotel** at Jack London Square (10 Washington St.; 510-836-3800, 800-729-3638; www.waterfrontplaza.com) is the only dockside hotel in these parts. The hotel is adjacent to the landing for ferries to San Francisco's Ferry Building and Fisherman's Wharf. Rooms facing the square are about $50 less than those with bay views.

▪▪▪▪ LOCAL CONTACT

Berkeley Convention and Visitors Bureau, visitors center at 2015 Center St.; 510-549-7040, 800-847-4823, www.visitberkeley .com. **Oakland Convention and Visitors Bureau**, 510-839-9000, www.oaklandcvbtravel.com.

15 · THE DELTA

Rio Vista, the southern gateway to the Delta, is about 60 miles from San Francisco. Take I-80 east to I-580, merging onto CA 24 toward Walnut Creek. Merge onto CA 242 north toward Concord, take CA 4 east toward Stockton, and then take CA 160 north.

Once you head east out of the San Francisco Bay Area and make your way across the Antioch Bridge, modern-day California—the strip malls, subdivisions, and traffic—fade away. You're in **the Delta**, a labyrinth of sloughs, channels, coves, and rivers, where old drawbridges swing open to let boats pass, ferries still run on cables, and in some places, the mailman comes by boat. The roads meander about the Sacramento River through tiny, slow-paced towns that haven't changed much in 50 years: Rio Vista, Isleton, Locke, Walnut Grove, and Ryde.

Like many other parts of Northern California, the history of the Delta is tied to the Gold Rush. The discovery of gold on the American River north of Sacramento sent thousands from San Francisco up the Sacramento River in paddle-wheeled steamboats. Some saw wealth of another kind in the rich soil of the Delta, if the river could be tamed. But

attempts to build levees by hand in the early 1850s failed. In the 1870s, new technology, the clamshell dredge, which scooped bottom mud and dropped it ashore, revolutionized levee building. At the same time, thousands of Chinese, having completed their task on the transcontinental railroad, were available for hire. Many settled in the Delta to help with levee construction and farming. By the time the Delta's reclamation was complete in the 1930s, some 550,000 acres, including 55 manufactured islands, had become farmland.

To get a flavor of life on those islands, head west from CA 160 on CA 12 over the Rio Vista Bridge. Take the first right, following signs to the **Ryer Island Ferry**. The diesel-powered vessel, *The Real McCoy*, dates from the 1940s and carries up to eight vehicles across the Sacramento River's deep-water channel. Operated by the California Department of Transportation, the free crossing takes four minutes each way.

From the ferry landing, turn right towards Ryde and head past **Snug Harbor**, a tree-shaded island, to another ferry, the *J. Mack,* which runs between Ryer Island and Grand Island. Once off the ferry, turn left on Grand Island Road and, about 3 miles north, you'll see **Grand Island Mansion**, a 58-room Italian villa with marble fireplaces, inlaid parquet flooring, and handmade tiles built by European craftsmen for orchard baron Louis Meyers. The villa is open for weddings and private events and on Sunday opens its doors to the general public for brunch (see "Where to Eat").

From Grand Island Road, head for Locke and Isleton. Go east on CA 220 a couple of miles and take CA 160 south as it winds along the tops of the levees, past acres of rice, grapes, and pear orchards spreading across the flat landscape below. Every couple of miles stand grand Victorian farmhouses, vestiges of early 20th-century farm life.

Locke is the most fascinating of the Delta towns. Established in 1915 by Chinese laborers, it has dozens of rickety wooden buildings lining its narrow lanes; the buildings' second-story balconies provide shade from the searing Central Valley sun. It's the only town in the U.S. built by Chinese people for Chinese people, although, sadly, the Alien Property Act prevented Chinese residents from owning the land under their buildings. Today, the entire town is on the National Register of Historic Places and, although still inhabited, feels like a ghost town. There are a couple of art galleries and restaurants (see "Where to Eat") and the **Dai Loy Museum**. The latter was once one of six old gambling houses where proprietors and players hurriedly closed up and fled whenever the marshals raided. Call ahead or check the Web (916-776-1661; www.locketown.com) for the museum's current opening hours.

Ten miles south from Locke along CA 160 is **Isleton**, a sleepy river town whose historic district is about four blocks long and includes art galleries, bait shops, and old buildings from the early 20th century. It is a quiet place except for Father's Day weekend in June, when the annual Crawdad Festival takes over Main Street (916-777-5880; www.crawdadfestival.org), in a celebration of the crustacean fished in Delta waters. So many folks—30,000 or so—show up for the festival that there aren't enough river lobsters to feed them; most of the crawdads are flown in from Louisiana.

The Delta's 1,000 miles of navigable and generally calm waterways make the area ideal for waterskiing and more. Windsurfers love the narrow channels where the westerly winds blow strong. Marinas throughout the Delta offer boat rentals for "gunkholing" —Delta slang for simply dropping anchor or tying up at unofficial moorages. Among the boat rental shops is **H2O To Go** (841 W. Brannan Island Rd., Isleton; 209-810-6755; www.H2Orents.com), which provides ski boats, fishing boats, WaveRunners, Jet Skis, and party boats by the hour or day. **Seven Crown Resorts** (Paradise Point Marina; 800-752-9669; www.sevencrown.com) is one of the largest outfits, renting fishing boats, ski boats, and houseboats, which are a leisurely way to explore the sleepy Delta waterways. Seven Crown's two-night rentals are the minimum, starting around $750 for a vessel that sleeps six. Houseboats are outfitted with full kitchens, bathrooms with a shower or tub, built-in bunks, and a gas barbecue. After an orientation, the length of which depends on how much boating experience you have, you are on your own and free to head to the Delta's many nooks and crannies. You can tie up at Isleton, Ryde, or Walnut Grove or explore the Meadows behind Locke where shade trees and beaches are found. On Little Potato Slough, small tule islands dot the waterways and provide nice spots to anchor.

Sunsets on the Delta are often gorgeous, as the wide, open sky erupts in strips of pink and orange. And when you've had your fill of peace and quiet and

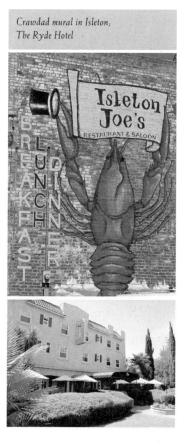

Crawdad mural in Isleton, The Ryde Hotel

nature, take a look at another wildlife experience in the marina bars and restaurants of Tower Park, Lost Isle, and other boaters-only spots, which turn into wild party scenes on summer afternoons.

Bird and nature lovers might want to plan their Delta trips on the first or third Saturday of the month when **Delta Ecotours** (916-775-4545; www.hartlandnursery.com) conducts two- to four-hour tours from Steamboat Slough near Grand Island. Tour leader Jeff Hart, a specialist in California habitat restoration, pilots the *Tule Queen II*, a 49-passenger catamaran. He covers the natural and human history of the region as well as water issues and environmental problems. Fall is the best time to view wildlife, especially ducks, geese, and songbirds. Any time of the year, you might see otters and minks.

▪▪▪▪ WHERE TO EAT

For a hearty breakfast, check out Isleton's local diner, the **River's Edge Cafe** (7 Main St.; 916-777-5723). The **Grand Island Mansion** (13415 Grand Island Rd., Walnut Grove; 916-775-2240; www.grandislandmansion.com) is open for Sunday champagne brunch from 10:30 AM to 2 PM.

Al's (13943 Main St., Locke; 916-776-1800), more commonly known as Al the Wop's, was the first Caucasian-run business in Locke. To say that owner Al Adami, who ran the place from 1934 to 1961, was a character is an understatement. He was known for putting thumbtacks in dollar bills and using a coin to toss them up to the ceiling, where they'd stick (a tradition that continues today); he'd also cut off men's neckties because he considered them too dressy. The saloon and restaurant is famous for its big steaks and pasta, which you eat seated on wooden benches at old tables.

There's nothing around quite like **Foster's Big Horn** (143 Main St., Rio Vista; 707-374-2511; www.fostersbighorn.com); animal lovers may be happy to hear that and avoid the place, while others will find it a kick. The bar and restaurant is packed with about 250 wild-game trophies—animals shot or trapped by former owner and bootlegger Bill Foster, who hunted big game in Africa, Canada, and Alaska. One trophy head is an African elephant, mounted in 1952. The moose over the bar has an antler spread of 76 inches. Photos along the walls tell of Foster's adventures. More tame is Rio Vista's **Point Waterfront Restaurant** (120 Marina Dr.; 707-374-5400; www.pointrestaurant.com), where sailboats and windsurfers scoot by as diners feast on roasted prime rib and rack of lamb.

▌▌▌▌ WHERE TO SLEEP

The salmon-colored **Ryde Hotel** (14340 Hwy. 160, Walnut Grove; 916-776-1318, 888-717-7933; www .rydehotel.com) is the place to stay in these parts, unless you're renting a houseboat. A Prohibition-era speakeasy dating from the late 1920s, the hotel has a fascinating history: It was once owned by Lon Chaney Jr. and in the 1970s was known for its rock 'n' roll bands. Art Deco in style, with ceiling fans, simply furnished rooms, and a cooling swimming pool out back, it's a wedding venue, so before you book, you may want to check whether any nuptial parties are going on.

▌▌▌▌ LOCAL CONTACT

California Delta Chambers and Visitors Bureau, 916-777-4041; www.californiadelta.org.

16 · SACRAMENTO

Sacramento is 90 miles northeast of San Francisco. Take I-80 east to US 50 east and take the downtown Sacramento exit.

Sacramento used to be written off as too hot, sprawling, and flat to be very interesting; it was only a place where schoolchildren were brought on field trips. But California's capital is now a flourishing city, and its downtown is energized with new museums and restaurants. There's even a midtown—on J Street between 22nd and 26th streets; the area would not be mistaken for New York City, but these blocks have an urban feel that's new for Sacramento.

There may be no better place to absorb California history than Sacramento, starting with **Capitol Park**, a lovely place to explore on foot. The park's 40 acres of lush lawns and gardens were laid out in the Victorian era, and most of parkland lies under a canopy of big elm trees, providing much-needed shade in the triple-digit summer heat. The **World Peace Rose Garden**, at 15th and L streets, is filled with a multiple variety of roses that bloom throughout the year.

The capitol itself is a beauty. The carefully restored Greco-Roman-style building (10th and L sts.; 866-240-4655; www.capitol museum.ca.gov), constructed from 1860 to 1874, is a panoply of frescoes and golf leaf. The legislative chambers are decorated with hand-painted ceilings and furnished with the original walnut desks from 1869. Guided tours are conducted on the hour each day. When the legislature is in session, visitors can watch government in action and maybe catch a glimpse of the state's famous actor-governor.

Sacramento has several fine museums well worth a look. One of the oldest in the western states is the **Crocker Art Museum** (216 O St.; 916-264-5423; www.crocker artmuseum.org), housed in a wedding-cake style 1885 Victorian. Its collection features many works by early California painters and dating from the Gold Rush.

At the **Leland Stanford Mansion** (800 N St.; 800-777-0369; www.lelandstanfordmansion.org), tours allow you to see the grand, 44-room home used by governors for official duties. Although today the governors don't actually live here, you can see the desk on which Governor Arnold Schwarzenegger may have signed a bill the day before. A $22 million renovation in 2005 restored the mansion to its glory days during the Victorian era when Leland Stanford, California's first governor (and founder of the university in Palo Alto), and two successive governors lived here. Original chandeliers from 1872 and 13 marble fireplaces are part of the décor.

This museum is not to be confused with the **Governor's Mansion** (1526 H St.; 916-323-3047; www.parks.ca.gov), where 13 of California's governors lived, from 1903 to 1967, when Ronald Reagan made his home here. It's another ornate Victorian home open for tours and filled with furnishings, marble fireplaces, and gubernatorial personal items, such as a bed extended to accommodate the six-feet-plus height of Governor Earl Warren (later chief justice of the U.S. Supreme Court).

The **California Museum for History, Women and the Arts** (1020 O St.; 916-653-7524; www.californiamuseum.org) was expanded in 2006 with a California Hall of Fame and a section devoted to trailblazing women. Among the displays are Sally Ride's space-flight suit and Peggy Fleming's Olympic gold medal. Other parts of the museum are dedicated to the state's history.

Three miles from downtown is **Sutter's Fort** (2701 L St.; 916-445-4422; www.parks.ca.gov), the first Anglo settlement in the Central Valley, founded by Swiss immigrant John Sutter in 1839. The blacksmith's shop and parts of Sutter's home provide a peek into pioneer farming life.

A 10-minute walk west from the capitol is the official western terminus of the Pony Express, today known as **Old Sacramento**, a 28-acre state historic park listed on the National Register of Historic Places. Well-preserved Gold Rush—era buildings, wooden sidewalks, and horse-drawn carriages add to the Old West flavor. Stop at the interpretive center (1002 2nd St.) to learn about the city's early transportation history. Nearby, the **Wells Fargo History Museum** (Second and J streets; 916-440-4263; www.wells fargohistory.com) details the bank's role in the Pony Express and stagecoach travel.

Even those who aren't railroad buffs enjoy the **California State Railroad Museum** (111 I St.; 916-445-6645; www.californiastaterailroadmuseum.org;), which holds 21 restored cars and locomotives, rail exhibits, and a gift shop with a mind-boggling array of rail-related books and music; if you're looking for CDs of train sounds, both steam and diesel, you'll find them here. To really hear and feel the chuffing and the hissing, clamber on board one of the old steam trains at the depot outside the museum for a 6-mile, 40-minute round-trip. They operate Saturdays and Sundays from April through September.

Next door, the **Discovery Museum's Gold Rush History Center** (101 I St.; 916-264-7057; www.thediscovery.org) recreates the steam-train era with a work-ing printing press from the time and interactive displays. A remarkable glass floor exhibits objects excavated from the old city.

When you've had enough of museums and want some fresh air, walk from Old Sacramento along the American River Parkway to **Discovery County Park**, a shady haven a mile away from the Gold Rush History Center, where the American River meets the Sacramento. Bicyclists may want to pedal the parkway's **Jedediah Smith Memorial Bicycle Trail** from Old Sac to Folsom Lake, 23 miles away. But bring your own bikes, for there aren't any rental shops in the area.

Sports fans will want to check out one of the country's most popular Triple-A baseball teams, the Sacramento River Cats, who play to enthusiastic crowds at **Raley Field**, just across the river from Old Sacramento.

Lovers of jazz should make it a point to visit Sacramento for the annual **Jazz Jubilee** (916-372-5277; www.sacjazz.com), which stretches for four syncopating days over Memorial Day weekend. It's the largest traditional jazz festival in the world, featuring mostly Dixieland, but also some swing, zydeco, and other modes. Concerts take place on 30 stages and nightclubs in downtown and

Old Sacramento, the state capitol, Sacramento

Old Sacramento. Make overnight arrangements months in advance to nab a room within walking distance of the venues.

▐▐▐▐ WHERE TO EAT

Sacramento's position on the Sacramento River is one of the city's most attractive features, and you can find a few good places to eat while watching the river roll by. One is **Joe's Crab Shack** (1210 Front St.; 916-553-4249; www.joescrabshack.com), a great place to enjoy water and bridge views while enjoying seafood. Downtown has many fine restaurants, including **Mikuni** (1530 J St.; 916-447-2111; www.mikunishushi.com), a high-end sushi palace, and **Zocalo** (1801 Capitol Ave.; 916-441-0303; www.zocalosacramento.com), an upscale Mexican restaurant with an often-packed outdoor patio. **Paragary's** (1401 28th St.; 916-457-5737; www.paragarys.com) is a local favorite for its pastas, grilled meats, and pizzas from a wood-burning oven. **Biba** (2801 Capitol Ave.; 916-455-2422; www.biba-restaurant.com) is a power-lunch and dinner spot, where politicians and lobbyists dine on cookbook author and chef Biba Caggiano's authentic Italian dishes. **Brew it Up!** (801 14th St.; 916-441-3000; www.brewitup.com) boasts the largest

selected of hand-crafted beers in town and is fun place for classic pub food. **Mulvaney's B&L** (1215 19 St.; 916-441-1771) opened in 2005 in a refurbished 1893 firehouse. It's been popular ever since, emphasizing local produce and dishes grandly conveyed out of an open kitchen into a boisterous dining room.

▐▐▐▐ WHERE TO SLEEP

For a city its size, Sacramento has the expected number of chain accommodations but surprisingly few small hotels and inns. Only a couple places downtown fit the bill. **The Inn at Parkside** (2116 Sixth St.; 916-658-1818, 800-995-7275; www.innatparkside.com) is a bed-and-breakfast with an elegant Asian atmosphere—no surprise since it once was the Chinese ambassador's home. The 11-room inn is lovingly furnished; its Tranquility Room is done in shades of blue, and the Spirit Room has a stunning wood-canopied bed with a mirror on the inside top of the canopy.

The **Amber House** (11315 22nd St.; 916-444-8085; www.amberhouse.com) is a charming inn in a 1905 Craftsman home with antiques-filled rooms named after writers; the Wordsworth has a deep whirlpool tub. Swiss-born owner Judith Bommer a few years ago expanded the inn into an

1895 Dutch Colonial home across the street, where rooms are named after musicians. The Mozart room is the most lavish, with a small patio and large Italian marble bathroom.

A unique experience is a night aboard the **Delta King** (1000 Front St.; 916-444-5464; www .deltaking.com), an authentic riverboat docked in Old Sacramento. It offers 44 staterooms, half facing the river and the other half the dock. The rooms are smallish, as expected on a boat, but they are fine for a night.

▮▮▮▮ LOCAL CONTACT

Sacramento Convention and Visitors Bureau, visitors center at 1002 Second St.; 916-808-7777; www.sacramentocvb.org.

HEADING EAST:

100 Miles and More from San Francisco

Yosemite Falls,
Yosemite National Park

PHOTO COURTESY OF YOSEMITE RESORTS

17 • AMADOR COUNTY

Jackson is about 120 miles east of San Francisco. Follow directions to Calaveras County (chapter 18) and, from CA 4 east in Stockton, merge onto CA 99 north. Then take CA 88 to Jackson.

Though named for an early rancher, this county has an apt name indeed: *Amador* means "love of gold" in Spanish. Just after gold was discovered in nearby El Dorado County, Andrew Kennedy struck it rich in what is today **Amador County**'s seat, Jackson, setting off a frenzy. The forty-niners arrived by the thousands. Dozens of mining camps sprouted and grew into towns, Plymouth, Sutter Creek, Volcano, Amador City, and Fiddletown among them. Today, they are quiet, well-preserved burgs linked by CA 49, which stretches the length of the Gold Country for 200 miles along the Sierra Nevada's western foothills. This road is an especially beautiful drive in the spring when the hills turn green and are carpeted with orange poppies.

Although the gold frenzy eventually died down, mining continued until 1942, when wartime priorities put a stop to it. In recent years, however, mining has resumed. At **Sutter Gold Mine** (13660 Hwy. 49, Sutter Creek; 866-762-2837; www.caverntours .com), visitors don hard hats and climb into mine cars. While it may seem like the start of a Disneyland ride, once underground there are no special effects. One of the guides, Charlie Chatfield—bearded, exuberant, funny—is straight from central casting. A fourth-generation miner, Chatfield compares the mining methods of today to the perilous techniques of old, when candles were used to light the way—sometimes igniting the natural methane gases underground—and drilling and blasting were carried on with a cavalier disregard for safety. Tours include the safe room, where miners congregate in case of a collapse, and a crouching walk through shafts being excavated. Lines of quartz containing gold can be spotted; by some estimates, 80 percent of the Amador gold that ever existed is still buried here.

Sutter Creek is among the prettiest of the Gold Country towns. Its stone buildings, Greek Revival homes, white picket fences, and church spires are reminiscent of New England. Main Street is lined with small shops, art galleries, and antiques stores. The **Sutter Creek Theatre** (4 Main St.; 877-547-6518; www.suttercreektheatre.com), built in 1912 as a silent film palace, today hosts plays, music, and comedy.

Take a side trip to **Volcano**, a charming village in a mountain valley full of history, even Civil War lore: its venerable cannon, Old Abe, on display in the center of town, was used by local Union militia to scare off Confederate sympathizers. You can walk around the tiny town (population less than 100) and soak up its well-preserved and noncommercialized Gold Rush atmosphere in less than an hour. The first theater group in California was formed here in 1856, and the show goes on at the **Cobblestone Theatre** (Volcano Theatre Company; 866-463-8650; www.volcanotheatre.org), whose stone walls date back to the theater's founding. Summer productions are performed in the amphitheater across the street. Have a drink at the Whisky Flats Saloon at the St. George Hotel (see "Where to Sleep") and check out the funky country store, which also serves as the local diner. There's no stove or oven: hamburgers are grilled in a Gold Rush–era chimney.

Another place to spend a couple of hours nosing around is **Amador City**, California's second smallest incorporated city (population 200); its short main drag has some of the best antiques shops in the region. The quaint **Amador Whitney Museum** (14170 Hwy. 49; 209-267-0928) focuses on the hard work of women and of various ethnic groups in the Gold Rush.

Jackson is bigger and more congested than its sleepier neighbors, but the historic center is fun to explore. The **Amador County Museum** (225 Church St.; 209-223-6386), housed in a two-story brick house dating from 1859, has a large-scale working model of the Kennedy Mine.

An intriguing picnic spot 1 mile north of town on Jackson Gate Road is the site of the Kennedy tailing wheels, remnants of massive wooden wheels once used to transport mine residue to a nearby dam. Across the road is the **Kennedy Mine** (209-223-9542; www.kennedygoldmine.com), where tours are available from March through October. Visitors can check out the museum and gift shop and the mine office, where gold flakes were melted into bricks to ship to San Francisco.

Amador is zinfandel wine country. California's earliest zinfandel vines were planted during the Gold Rush. It's a variety native to Croatia but has been grown by Italians and other ethnic groups here in the **Shenandoah Valley**, an area of hilly terrain northeast of tiny town of Plymouth. Early pioneers gave Shenandoah its name when the green hills of spring reminded them of Virginia's Blue Ridge Valley. The pace is unhurried here at 35 wineries, which have no tasting fees and less attitude than California's better-known wine regions. So even if you don't know your zin from your merlot, you'll feel quite comfortable.

Sobon Estate (14330 Shenandoah Rd.; Plymouth; 209-245-6554; www.sobonwine.com) dates back to 1856 and operated even during Prohibition, when it made sacramental wine. The estate includes a museum in the original winery building. Try the earthy, full-bodied zinfandels, such as the Fiddletown. Another acclaimed winery is **Renwood** (12225 Steiner Rd.; 209-245-6979; www.renwood.com) with its famous zins and barberas. For a map and winery listing, contact Amador County Vintners at 888-655-8614 (www.amadorwine.com).

Six miles east of Plymouth is the community of **Fiddletown**, established in 1849 by a group of Missourians described as "always fiddling." The home of a thriving Chinese population during the Gold Rush, a relic of the era is the **Chew Kee Store**, a rammed-earth building with 12-inch walls that has been lovingly brought back to life through a community effort. It now houses a small museum open only on Saturday, from April through October (www.fiddletown.info).

For a few weeks in spring, Amador's main destination is **Daffodil Hill**, a postcard-perfect ranch set amid pine forests 12 miles above Sutter Creek, off Pine Grove-Volcano Road. It is owned by the McLaughlins, a fifth-generation pioneer ranching family who plants hundreds of daffodil bulbs each year. Nature sets the schedule, but generally from late March through the first three weeks of April, an estimated 300,000 daffodils—more than three hundred varieties—emerge in the sunshine covering four acres. The McLauglins charge no admission fee, but donations are accepted. Call 209-296-7048 for a visitation schedule.

Higher up in the Sierra, along scenic CA 88 about 50 miles east of Jackson, are the stunning Silver and Caples lakes. The two alpine lakes are near 8,650-foot **Carson Pass**, which was originally part of the Emigrant Trail trav-

The St. George Hotel, Volcano

Chew Kee Store, Fiddletown

eled by thousands of fortune seekers on their way to the gold fields. Short day hikes, such as the Little Round Top trail, a 2¹⁄₂-mile romp through forest and meadow, lead to granite lakes with awesome wildflower viewing. For a side trip and stunning panoramic views, climb to the 9,500-foot summit of Round Top. For the Little Round Top trailhead, make a right off CA 88 at the Cal Trans Maintenance Station near Caples Lake and drive 2 miles to the parking lot.

■ ■ ■ ■ WHERE TO EAT

The patio at the **Sutter Creek Coffee Company** (20 Eureka St.; 888-219-4127; www.suttercreek coffeeco.com) is a sunny place to rest weary feet, enjoy a sandwich and fresh-roasted coffee, and read a variety of newspapers. In Amador City, **Andrae's Bakery and Cheese Shop** (14141 Hwy. 41; 209-267-1352; www.andraes bakery.com) serves sandwiches made from its own hearth-baked, organic-flour bread. Try the Basque cake, a specialty. Nearby, the **Imperial Hotel** (14202 Hwy. 49; 209-267-9172; www.imperial amador.com) houses an elegant, white tablecloth restaurant with a menu featuring local organic products. Diners drive for miles to reach **Taste** (9402 Main St., Plymouth; 209-245-3463; www .restauranttaste.com), which serves high-quality food in the sleek atmosphere of a hip San Francisco restaurant but at half the price.

■ ■ ■ ■ WHERE TO SLEEP

The **Sutter Creek Inn** (75 Main St.; 209-267-5606; www.sutter creekinn.com) looks like something out of a Thomas Kinkade painting—and indeed it is. (The painting's title is *The Village Inn*.) Owner Jane Way created this nostalgic hideaway 40 years ago and has since updated it with rooms in renovated outbuildings. The Tool Shed, for instance, has a wood-burning fireplace and a bed that hangs from cables from the ceiling; one slumbers as if on a gently rocking boat. The gardens are a serene sanctuary.

The **Hanford House** (61 Hanford St., Sutter Creek; 209-267-0747; 800-871-5839; www.hanfordhouse.com) is a luxurious, ivy-covered red-brick inn with large suites, such as number 4, which has a fireplace and private terrace. Even the smallest of the inn's rooms, the Blue Room, is quite sizeable.

Volcano has one of the most evocative Gold Country inns, the **St. George Hotel** (16104 Main St.; 209-296-4458; www.stgeorgehotel.com), which has been welcoming travelers since 1862. Rooms in the historic building have shared baths, but those in the annex have private bathrooms. Prices are under $100 for a room with shared bath; book the Dogtown Room, which is the largest. The hotel's separate Garden Cottage is a good value for under $200. Guests gather in the adjacent Whiskey Flats Saloon, a funky bar often lively with music.

▌▌▌▌ LOCAL CONTACT

Amador County Chamber of Commerce, visitors center at intersection of CA 49 and CA 88, Jackson; 209-223-0350, www.amadorcountychamber.com.

18 • CALAVERAS COUNTY

Angels Camp is about 130 miles east San Francisco. Take I-80 east to CA 24 and then take I-205 east, which merges onto I-5 north, toward Stockton. Take the downtown Stockton exit, which merges to CA 4 east, leading to Angels Camp.

Not much would be known about **Calaveras County** if it weren't for a frog named Daniel Webster. As the story goes, miners who crowded into the county's biggest town, Angels Camp, during the Gold Rush didn't have much to do in their off hours. One of them got a frog to start jumping, then bet against another miner and his hopping frog, and the wagers flew.

Of course, these frogs would have been lost in history if it weren't for Mark Twain who, in the fall of 1865, visited Angels Camp. He wrote about Jim Smiley, who carried his frog, Daniel Webster, around town in a basket under his arm, boasting Webster was the "best jumper." When Twain's story *The Celebrated Jumping Frog of Calaveras County* was printed later that year, Angels Camp became world famous.

Stop by the visitors center (see "Local Contact") for a walking map and take an enjoyable tromp around town. Cross the Angels Creek footbridge and step up the "chicken ladder" on Hardscrabble Street, constructed on a steep slope. Check out **Turners Wild West** (1235 Main St.), which has an assortment of rodeo gear and cowboy hats. You can imagine the sound of noisy saloons on Main Street and picture dance halls and the bustle of the miners at the 1855-era **Angels Hotel**, where Mark Twain reportedly first heard about the frog.

Twain's tale is the focal point of the annual Calaveras County Fair and Jumping Frog Jubilee, which draws thousands to Angels Camp on the third weekend in May (209-736-2561; www.frog town.org). For a small fee you can rent your own frog for the day and enter it—becoming a jockey, in local parlance—in the competition. The world-record jump is just over 21 feet.

Hundreds of limestone caverns lie under the rolling hills of Calaveras County, and three examples are open to the public. **Moaning Caverns** (5350 Moaning Cave Rd.; Vallecito; 209-736-2708; www.caverntours.com), just 4 miles east of Angels Camp, is a deep limestone cavern 16 stories high (large enough to hold the Statue of Liberty); it is reached by a spiral staircase with more than 200 steps—not for anyone with bad knees or vertigo. Guides describe the history and geology of the cavern, telling gripping stories of how the first miners tied one end of a rope to a tree, fastened the rope around their waists, and crawled down the cavern's small opening by candlelight. Tour guides turn off the lights to show what happened when the miners' candles blew out. They point out the Igloo, a calcite stalagmite that is two stories tall and 5,000 years old, that looks like a spooky space alien. More athletic visitors can try the rappel option, in which they descend 165 feet by rope into the main chamber. No experience is necessary, and gloves, hard hat, and equipment are provided. The more adventurous (and not claustrophobic) can take a guided tour that uses lighted helmets and delves into deeper, unlighted parts of the cavern.

California Cavern (Cave City Road off Mountain Ranch; 209-736-2708; www.caverntours.com)

is an expansive underground complex of large rooms, miles of winding passes, and deep lakes. It takes over an hour to cover the lighted trails. More challenging are guided trips in which participants don coveralls and lighted helmets to walk across underground lakes and through deep passageways. Another nearby cave is **Mercer Caverns** (1665 Sheep Ranch Rd., Murphys; 209-728-2101; www.mercercaverns .com), which has a large variety of unusual crystalline formations, including some that are frostlike white crystal.

From Angels Camp, drive 9 miles east on CA 4 to another mining town, **Murphys**, one of

Rappelling in Moaning Caverns

the best-preserved Gold Rush burgs. Its streets are lined with old oaks and cedars and handsome buildings from the late 1800s. It's a lively town that's not overrun with kitschy shops, perhaps because, unlike other Mother Lode towns, it's on a side street off the highway.

A picturesque creekside park with a gazebo is where the pokey —a real old-time, two-room jail— still stands. You'll soon pick up on a fact of Gold Rush history: fires were common in the pioneer days, and shabby wooden structures that easily burned were often replaced with buildings of rock walls and iron doors. You can see many of those rock buildings, such as the Murphys Hotel (see "Where to Sleep"), still standing. Take a look in the **Old Timers Museum** (470 Main St.; 728-1160) to see Gold Rush memorabilia. On the wall outside plaques, some wacky, hang on the Wall of Comparative Ovations, established by E. Clampus Vitus, the quirky fraternal order devoted to preserving western U.S. history. Stroll over to the old Protestant and Catholic cemeteries, on opposite hills of the town, and wander among faded, Gold Rush—era tombstones marking the graves of early settlers. There's just enough detail—date of birth and place of birth—to

make your heartstrings tug for the short lives that ended so far from home.

Calaveras County is full of natural wonders, including the beauty of the world's tallest trees: the giant sequoias. Fourteen miles east of Murphys, past the town of Arnold, is **Calaveras Big Trees State Park** (Hwy. 4; 209-795-2334; www.parks.ca.gov). The park has two groves of the magnificent trees that rise up to 325 feet in height and have diameters of 30 feet; it also includes 6,000 acres of pine forest. Miles of hiking and bicycling trails are marked for wintertime crosscountry skiing and snowshoeing. The Stanislaus River runs through the park, offering a place to cool off in pools in summer. Stop at the visitors center to get a map and walk the easy 1½-mile North Grove loop trail. Or hike the 5-mile loop trail in the denser, less-traveled South Grove and see more giants, including the 250-foot Agassiz (25 feet in diameter 6 feet off the ground), the largest tree in the park.

No talk of travel in Calaveras County would be complete without mention of the burgeoning wine industry. You can sample several wines by simply strolling Murphys' Main Street, where several wineries (Millaire, Twisted Oak, Zucca Mountain among them) have tasting rooms, or you can head into the surrounding countryside. Winery staffs here proudly mention that, unlike other California wine areas, Calaveras wineries charge no tasting fees.

None of the wineries are large, and some make just 3,000 cases a year. The exception is **Ironstone Vineyards** (1894 Six Mile Rd.; 209-728-1251; www.ironstone vineyards.com), which produces 300,000 cases. It has the most lavish winery, with lovely grounds, and offers free tastings and tours. An outdoor amphitheater hosts summer concerts by well-known artists (Vince Gill and B. B. King were among the performers in 2007). A stunning 44-pound crystalline gold specimen—said to be priceless in value—from a local mine is on display. A gourmet deli sells sandwiches and other goodies, and there's a park by a pond and gardens to picnic in.

Stevenot (2690 San Domingo Rd.; 209) 728-0638; www.stevenot winery.com) is more down-to-earth. Its barnlike tasting room, tucked in a canyon near Murphys, has a big stone fireplace. It is the county's oldest winery, dating only from the 1970s. A grape arbor shades a cozy picnic area.

Awesome Sierra landscapes await those who drive about 30 miles east of Murphys along CA 4 to higher elevations in the Sierra Nevada. **Sierra Nevada Adventure Company** (2293 Hwy. 4; 209-795-9310; www.snacattack.com) in Arnold rents kayaks and canoes for use at several nearby reservoirs and lakes, including beautiful Lake Alpine.

For a more remote wilderness experience, take the canoes or kayaks to **Spicer Reservoir**, a pristine lake at the base of the Dardanelles volcanic range. (From Arnold, take CA 4 east to Spicer Reservoir Road turnoff—about an hour drive.) In the Bear Valley resort area on CA 4, the **Bear Valley Adventure Company** (209-753-2834; www.bearvalley xc.com) also rents bikes and kayaks. Both shops rent winter sports equipment as well and provide lots of information on local wilderness areas to explore.

Back at lower elevations, another Gold Rush town awaits, this one on CA 49 on the northern edge of Calaveras County, near the border of Amador County. **Mokelumne Hill** (shortened by locals to "Moke Hill") is just a speck on the map today, but it was once one of the principal mining towns in the state. The bar at the Hotel Leger (see "Where to Sleep") was once known as one of the rowdiest in the Gold Country. Today, Moke Hill a quiet town with boarded-up old Gold Rush buildings waiting for makeovers and whitewashed old churches, including the oldest church in the state: the First Congregational Church, erected in 1856.

■ ■ ■ ■ WHERE TO EAT

The **Pickle Barrel** (1225 S. Main St.; 209-736-4704; www.picklebarrel.com), in the middle of historic Angels Camp, is an old-fashioned lunch spot that serves grilled sandwiches made from meat barbecued out back. Murphys has the best selection of places to eat, starting with a quick breakfast spot: **Aria Bakery** (458 Main St.; 209-728-9250; www.ariabakery.com) bakes croissants, breads, and pastries each morning and has an espresso bar. The **Alchemy Market** (191 Main St.; 209-728-0700; www.alchemymarket.com) is a high-end deli and cafe that is the perfect place to stock up for a picnic or a quick lunch. Another casual eatery is **Firewood** (420 Main St.; 209-728-3248), which serves not only pizza, cooked blistering hot in its Italian wood-burning oven, but also, incongruously, tacos and other Mexican food. The classiest bar and most sophisticated menu around can be found at **V Restaurant and Bar** (402-H Main St.; 209-728-0107); the chef, who used to head the kitchen at Yosemite's Awhwahnee Hotel, creates large and small plates of Mediterranean-style cuisine.

■ ■ ■ ■ WHERE TO SLEEP

The oldest continually operating hotel in California is the **Murphys Hotel** (457 Main St.; 209-728-3444; 800-532-7684; www.murphyshotel.com), dating from 1859. Its creaky floors show its age, but where else can you sleep in the bed where President

The gardens at Ironstone Vineyards

Ulysses S. Grant once slept—and pay less than $100 to do so? Mark Twain, Horatio Alger, and Susan B. Anthony were some of the hotel's other illustrious guests. Showers and toilets are down in the hall in linoleum-floored, closet-sized bathrooms (even the Grant "presidential suite" shares a bath). A 1950s and '60s annex has updated, motel-style rooms with private baths and modern amenities such as TVs with cable.

For much more luxury, try the **Dunbar House** (271 Jones St.; 209-728-2897; 800-692-6006; www.dunbarhouse.com) a couple of blocks away—a bed-and-breakfast in an opulent 1880 Victorian, surrounded by lush landscaped gardens. Among the lavish rooms is the Sequoia, the former library off of the breakfast room, which has a seating area and two-person whirlpool tub. The least expensive but spacious

Blue Oak room has a queen bed under the sloping ceiling of the attic.

Mokelumne Hill is the home of the **Hotel Leger** (8304 Main St.; 209-286-1401; www.hotelleger.com), parts of which date to 1851. With tipsy old floors, Victorian furniture, and a wraparound balcony, it is a pleasant place to watch the world go by. Rooms 1 and 2 have balcony access, private baths, and quaint old wood-burning fireplaces. Be on the lookout for the resident ghost. The hotel restaurant and Gold Rush—era bar regularly have live music.

■ ■ ■ ■ LOCAL CONTACT

Calaveras County Visitors Bureau, visitors center at 1192 South Main St., Angels Camp; 209-736-0049; www.gocalaveras.com.

19 · NEVADA CITY & GRASS VALLEY

Nevada City is about 150 miles northeast of San Francisco. From Sacramento (see chapter 16), continue on I-80 east and, at Auburn, take CA 49 north.

Nevada City was once the largest and most prosperous of all the Gold Rush boomtowns; miners collected a pound of gold a day from Deer Creek, the stream that trickles through town. Today, Nevada City is a well-preserved relic of that era; the entire downtown listed on the National Register of Historic Places. It's more than a museum, however. Prosperous once more, the place thrives on tourist trade and a real estate industry catering to retirees and high-tech workers settling in this idyllic area.

Unlike many of Northern California's once boisterous Gold Rush towns, which now have their sidewalks rolled up by 8 PM, Nevada City has a lively nightlife and cultural scene because of the musicians, artists, and writers who are drawn here. Live music can be found in bars and restaurants all over town. To get a flavor of the place, tune into Nevada City's radio station, KVMR (89.5 FM), for its quirky selection of music (*The Tibetan Radio Hour* and *Patchouli Haze* are two programs), local news, and talk by personalities such as Travus T. Hipp. For live music every night, there's **Friar Tuck's** (III N. Pine St.; 503-265-9093; www.friar tucks.com). For concerts and plays, check out the **Miners Foundry Cultural Center** (325 Spring St.; 530-265-5040; www .minersfoundry.org). At the hamlet of Rough and Ready, a short drive west of neighboring Grass Valley, a Sunday morning jam session of local musicians, called the **Fruit Jar Pickers**, is open to the public (Opry Palace; 530-432-1501; www.fruitjarpickers.com).

Surrounded by lovely neighborhoods of Victorian homes on seven hills, Nevada City's historic district is lined with restored gaslights and filled with art galleries and boutiques. Stop in at the visitors center (see "Local Contact") for a detailed walking map, which describes many of the town's 93 historic buildings.

Historic Firehouse #1 on Main Street, Nevada City

The Holbrooke Hotel, Grass Valley

Among them are the **Nevada Theatre** (401 Broad St.), opened in 1865 and where Mark Twain once gave a presentation, and the **Methodist Church** (433 Broad St.), built in 1869. Take a stroll from the **National Hotel** (211 Broad St.) up Broad Street to where the street splits and follow

East Broad, then return on the street's opposite side for a look at one of the town's prettiest residential neighborhoods.

It's surprising to discover that Nevada City's peak season is not summer, as in most of the Gold Country, or fall when the foliage is stunning, but two weeks in December, when the town is decked out for Victorian Christmas Days in celebration of the original settlers from the British Isles. Horse-drawn carriages, lavishly decorated trees, and thousands of sparkling white lights set the stage. Local bed-and-breakfast inns are booked up at least a month prior to the event.

Summer finds locals heading 5 miles from Nevada City to **Scotts Flat Lake**, a reservoir with a sandy swimming beach in a forested valley. At the lake marina (23333 Scotts Flat Rd.; 530-265-8861; www.aboutnevada county.com.), kayaks, canoes, and motorboats are available for rent.

Other local swimming holes are 6 miles northwest of Nevada City on CA 49, along the South Fork of the Yuba River, where huge granite boulders create delightful natural pools. Park in the lot at the CA 49 bridge. The pools draw a crowd scene on hot summer days, but they are worth a trip.

The entire area is part of **South**

Yuba River State Park (530-432-2546; www.parks.ca.gov), which extends 20 miles along the Yuba. A moderate walk that provides a glimpse into the impressive engineering feats of the forty-niners is the Independence Trail. This 5-mile loop takes you along ridges, over gorges, and past old wooden canals and aqueducts (called *flumes* by the miners), not to mention several tempting swimming holes. The parking lot and trailhead is about ¼ mile south of the CA 49 bridge.

The park also includes the old Bridgeport mining camp and visitors center on a stretch of the river where some of the richest gold deposits were found. The main attraction is a 229-foot covered bridge, dating from 1862, that once knew the clatter and rumble of Wells Fargo wagons and is thought to be the longest covered and arched single span bridge in existence. To get to the mining camp from the CA 49 bridge, continue north on CA 49 for several twisty, hilly miles and take a left at Pleasant Valley Road.

Just as filled with history as Nevada City is **Grass Valley**, the "working class" neighboring Gold Rush town (the miners lived here, their bosses in Nevada City), 4 miles south on CA 49. Here you'll find Cornish pasties (pronounced *PASS-tees*) at several outlets, including Marshall's (203 Mill St.). Biting into one of these doughy meat pies is a taste of Gold Rush history: miners from England's Cornwall region put a couple in their lunch bins before heading down into the mines each day.

Stop at the visitors center (see "Local Contact") for a walking-tour map of downtown. The tour starts at the center's **Lola Montez house**, a replica of the home of this world-famous performer. The oak tree outside is where votes were collected in a cigar box for the first town election in 1850. Montez's neighbor, Lotta Crabtree, entertained at mining camps and was the first American singer and dancer to become a millionaire; her house is at 238 Mill Street. Peek in at the **Holbrooke Hotel** (212 W. Main St.), a Gold Rush saloon and hotel rebuilt with stone and brick after the town's disastrous fire of 1855. One of Grass Valley's best-known landmarks, it has been restored to its original splendor.

Nevada City and Grass Valley jointly promote themselves as "Booktown." The towns' nearly two dozen independent booksellers include two in Grass Valley: **Booktown Books** (107 Bank St.; 530-272-4655;www.booktown books.com), a co-op of independent booksellers that has more than 30,000 volumes under one roof, and **Ames Bookstore** (309 Neal St.; 530-273-9261), which has 300,000 volumes and is one of the largest used bookstores in California.

Hardrock (underground) mining was dominant in Grass Valley until World War II. The most successful mine, once the richest in the state, operated until 1956 and is today **Empire Mine State Historic Park** (10791 E. Empire St.; 530-273-8522; www.empiremine .org). The story of the 367 miles of underground passages dug by Cornishmen, considered the finest hardrock miners in the world, and the unique system of steam-operated pumps they used, is fascinating. You can see the mine office, machine shop, and other buildings on your self-guided tour. Also available are tours of the owner's idyllic 1897 English-stone mansion and lovingly tended rose garden. A 2-mile loop hike along the Hardrock Trail starts from the park's main parking lot and passes many historic mining sites. Trail maps are available at the park's visitors center.

▪▪▪▪ WHERE TO EAT

Breakfast places are abundant in Nevada City. **Posh Nosh** (318 Broad St.; 530-265-6064;) offers many creative varieties of eggs benedict. **Ike's Quarter Cafe** (401 Commercial St.; 503-265-6138) has a shady patio—a pleasant place to linger on a warm day—and breakfast or lunch with a flavor of New Orleans; gumbo is always on the menu. **Cafe Mecca** (237 Commercial St.; 530-478-1517), with its range of desserts made by a Belgian pastry chef, is an inviting coffeehouse for chocolate lovers as well as coffee addicts and laptop users. For dinner, the most acclaimed spot in town is **Citronee** (320 Broad St.; 530-265-5697; www.citronee bistro.com), which serves American cuisine with a Mediterranean influence. Citronee also has a deli that is a good place to buy picnic supplies. **New Moon Cafe** (203 York St.; 530-265-6399; www.the newmooncafe.com) specializes in organic local ingredients; its menu includes homemade bread and ice cream. **The Stonehouse** (107 Sacramento St.; 530-265-5050; www.stonehouse1857.com), located in a cavelike 19th-century brewery built from local stone, serves succulent rotisserie chicken from a wood-burning oven.

▪▪▪▪ WHERE TO SLEEP

Nevada City and Grass Valley have a good selection of inns and bed-and-breakfasts, most in beautiful old homes. The **Emma**

Nevada House (528 E. Broad St.; 530-265-4415, 800-916-EMMA; www.emmanevadahouse.com) is a picture-perfect restored 1856 Victorian in a quiet location. It has a century-old cherry tree rising out in the middle of its lovely large backyard deck. The Empress Chamber, with a whirlpool tub, is the most romantic room; cozy Palmer's Loft has the home's original claw-foot tub.

The **Outside Inn** (575 E. Broad St.; 530-265-2233; www.outside inn.com), as the name implies, is geared to outdoorsy types. One room even has a rock-climbing wall. Originally an old-fashioned, 1940s motor court, it was renovated in the last 10 years. Some of the rooms, including the cheery Winter Room, still have their original knotty pine walls. You can't beat relaxing on the pretty creekside patio on a warm summer evening.

The **Red Castle Inn** (109 Prospect St.; 530-265-5135, 800-761-4766; www.redcastleinn .com), one of California's first bed-and-breakfast establishments, is a beautifully furnished retreat on a hill close to town. The front parlor and spacious sitting room are done up with Oriental rugs, gorgeous antiques, and shelves of books. The Garden Room, with a reproduction canopy bed, and the Rose Room, with a large private veranda, are favorites. The large Forest View Room, which has a private entrance and claw-foot tub, may be one of the best values around, offering a lot of romance at a relatively reasonable rate of less than $200 per night.

Annie Horan's (415 W. Main St., Grass Valley; 530-272-1516; www.anniehoran.com) is a warm and inviting Victorian bed-and-breakfast within walking distance of Grass Valley's restaurants and shops. Though furnished with handsome Victorian pieces, the décor is pleasantly nonfrilly. Annie's Room is the largest and has a bathroom featuring a full-size claw-foot tub.

▪▪▪▪ LOCAL CONTACT

Nevada City Chamber of Commerce, visitors center at 132 Main St., 530-265-2692, www.nevada citychamber.com. **Grass Valley/ Nevada County Chamber of Commerce**, visitors center at 248 Mill St., 530-273-4667, 800-655-4667; www.grassvalleychamber .com.

20 · DOWNIEVILLE

Downieville is about 188 miles north San Francisco. Follow directions to Nevada City (chapter 19) and continue on CA 49 north.

If you're a mountain biker, you've probably heard about **Downieville**. For the last 10 years, thousands of riders have swarmed this tiny town in the foothills above Nevada City one week in mid-July for the Downieville Classic Mountain Bike Festival. The highlights are bike races that draw 200 downhill riders and 600 cross-country riders (plus some daredevils launched from a wooden ramp into the rivers). It's quite a contrast to the rest of the year when the little village of 19th-century wooden and brick buildings seems downright sleepy. Becoming a bikers' mecca has not changed Downieville much, except for one gleaming bike shop that looks as if it were plucked off a street in Marin County.

For nonbikers, there isn't much to do in Downieville, population 325, except to soak up its Gold Rush atmosphere. But its lush setting in a steep, forested canyon at the meeting point of two rapid-flowing rivers—the Downie and the North Fork of the Yuba River—makes the town a peaceful place to loaf for a spell.

The town is named after Major William Downie, a Scottish immigrant who came to California after gold was discovered. Legend has it that Downie and a party of men camped at a spot on the Yuba where they found gold in the bottom of the pan in which they had cooked a large trout. The news spread, and miners poured into town, then known as the Forks, which became a bustling nexus of gold camps that stretched out along the rivers. (One of the largest pieces of gold found in the region—a mass weighing precisely 5,009 ounces and valued at $84,300 at the time—was unearthed near Downieville in 1852.) In 1850 the population of 2,000 agreed to change the name to Downieville after the major. It became the county seat of Sierra County in 1852.

The **Downieville Museum** (330 Main St.; 530-289-3194), located in an 1852 store built of local stone by Chinese immigrants, contains displays that show life in the Gold Rush days; the collections include mining tools, Indian artifacts, and household articles. It's closed November through mid-April. For a more personal feel of the history, take a walk past Pauly Creek Falls to the town cemetery and see the miners' graves from the 1850s.

You can also experience the reason bikers flock to Downieville. Two mountain bike specialists, **Downieville Outfitters** (530-289-0155; www.downieville outfitters.com) and **Yuba Expeditions** (530-289-3010; www .yubaexpeditions.com)—that's the gleaming one—offer rentals. They shuttle riders to Packer Saddle, up near the spectacular mountain outcropping called the Sierra Buttes. There, on three different old mining routes, once used by oxen and mules to transport supplies, riders have a choice of trails to take down back to Downieville. Rides typically take two or three hours and travel through rugged mountain forests.

Others may want to instead simply lounge by the river with a good book.

▌▌▌▌ WHERE TO EAT

Downieville's restaurant selection is small. The **Grubstake Saloon** (315 Main St.; 530-289-0289) serves a variety of burgers for lunch and steak for dinner. If you're staying at a place with a small kitchen and a barbecue, the dearth of restaurants isn't a problem. Head to the general store in Downieville and stock up on supplies.

Or drive 9 miles north along the Yuba to another historic Gold Rush town, Sierra City, which has a bigger selection of eateries. For breakfast and lunch there's the friendly, old-fashioned **Red Moose Cafe** (224 Main St.; 530-862-1502). For dinner, **Herrington's Sierra Pines** (101 Main St.;

The Yuba River flows past the Sierra Shangri-La.

530-862-1151, 800-682-9848; www.herringtonssierrapines.com) has been a favorite of the martini-and-prime-rib crowd for generations. Trout from its pond is also on the menu.

▮▮▮▮ WHERE TO SLEEP

If you're looking for luxury, look elsewhere. But if you're looking for comfortable accommodations and tranquility, several places here offer it, including two Yuba River resorts that have catered for years to trout fishermen. The **Lure Resort** (Hwy. 49; 530-289-3465, 800-671-4084; www.lureresort .com) is reached by a narrow suspension bridge from the highway just outside town. Several knotty-pine cabins, renovated in the last few years, are nestled amid pines, firs, oaks, and cedars. Cabin II is a nice example of the resort's comfy amenities, offering a stone-encircled gas fireplace, full kitchen, and deck overlooking the rushing river.

The charming **Sierra Shangri-La** (Hwy. 49; 530-289-3455; www .sierrashangrila.com) did not get its name because of its idyllic setting but from a sheer rock wall on the nearby Yuba. This hotel is a place to hibernate and lounge on lush lawns overlooking a curve in the river. The cottages are the epitome of cozy, particularly the Jim Crow (named after the man who cooked the trout in the pan where gold was found), a studio unit with a deck over the river and a full kitchen. The Flycaster, newly remodeled with a stone fireplace, has a deck set over the rushing waters. Three hotel-style rooms without kitchens are for rent over the main lodge.

▮▮▮▮ LOCAL CONTACT

Sierra County Chamber of Commerce, 800-200-4949, www .sierracounty.org.

21 · YOSEMITE NATIONAL PARK

Yosemite National Park is 195 miles east of San Francisco. Take I-80 east to CA 580 east, following signs for Tracy/Stockton to CA 205. Follow CA 205 east and take Highway 120 east to the park entrance, which is about an hour's drive from the Yosemite Valley.

When John Muir came to Yosemite in 1868, he described the experience in rapturous terms. "Divine peace glows on all the majestic landscape like the silent enthusiastic joy that sometimes transfigures a noble human face," he wrote in his journal on an August day. Muir spent an entire summer in the Sierra that year; a much shorter stay, however, is enough time for visitors to fall into a similar reverie.

Yosemite National Park's 7-mile-long, glacier-carved valley is full of icons: Yosemite Falls, El Capitan, Half Dome, Cathedral Rocks, Sentinel Dome among them. Individually, they are awe-inspiring. Taken together, they are almost overwhelming.

Every season has something in its favor: Winter has the quiet beauty of meadows and granite peaks dusted white. Spring has dogwood blooms and the roaring fullness of the waterfalls. Summer offers the warmth of the sun and long days. In the autumn months, waterfalls are only trickles, but the crowds are gone and the maples and oaks turn to red and gold. Summer draws the most of the park's four million annual visitors, but if you hit the trails in the early morning, even some of the park's most visited spots, such as 2,425-foot **Yosemite Falls**, the tallest waterfall in North America, will seem like yours alone.

Two-hour valley tours, by bus in winter and open-air tram in summer, provide a convenient introduction. They stop to allow photography as rangers describe the park's history, geology, and nature. The stops include **Tunnel View**, which offers a postcard-perfect panorama. The tours leave several times a day from Yosemite Lodge. (For tour and activity reservations and information, call 209-372-1240 or check out www.yosemitepark .com.)

Organizing your own visit to the valley is relatively easy. Pick up a copy of *Yosemite Today* at park entrances to see what is on tap for the day and evening. There's always a variety of ranger-led educational walks, photography seminars, or evening nature- or star-gazing programs. The free Yosemite Valley shuttle bus runs year-round from 7 AM to 10 PM (every 5 or 10 minutes in summer, about every 15 minutes in winter); visitors can hop on and off at 21 points in the valley.

Whether it's your first visit to Yosemite or your 15th, there are certain musts: walking the ½-mile paved trail to the observation area at the base of **Lower Yosemite Falls** is one. Stopping at the meadow in front of **El Capitan** and gazing at the antlike progress of climbers on the 3,000-foot granite monolith is another. The possibilities for day hikes—and the payoff of breathtaking sights—are many. See the National Park Service's Web site (see "Local Contact") for several suggestions.

The classic hike is **Mist Trail** to Vernal and Nevada falls. Take the shuttle to the Happy Isles stop or walk the ½ mile from Curry Village to Happy Isles. From Happy Isles, take Mist Trail to the **Vernal Falls** bridge. The section from here to the top of Vernal is a bit perilous if you're not prepared.

The trail is slippery from the cool spray, which will get you wet in the spring and early summer. Make sure you wear thick-soled shoes with good traction for the climb up 600 steep granite steps. From the top, it is a short walk to Emerald Pool and then another 1,100-foot climb to the top of **Nevada Falls**. If that's too much, take the trail at the top of Vernal to **Clark Point** and follow the signs for the less-strenuous **John Muir Trail** back down to Yosemite Valley, a path that's easier on your knees than the Mist Trail.

About 12 miles of dedicated bike paths crisscross the eastern end of Yosemite Valley. Bike rentals are available from late spring to late fall at Yosemite Lodge and Curry Village. The bike paths wind along the valley highlights, including Yosemite Village, Yosemite Falls, several meadows, and Merced River beaches.

At Yosemite Village, there's a visitors center and the **Ansel Adams Gallery** and gift shop (209-372-4413; www.anseladams.com), the latter full of special-edition prints and books dedicated to the black-and-white masterpieces of photographer Ansel Adams. The nearby **Yosemite Museum** covers local Miwok and Paiute tribal culture and offers basket-weaving demonstrations.

A re-created Native American village is behind the museum.

If you're not staying or dining at **the Ahwahnee**, make sure to visit. This 1927 hotel is a national historic landmark and one of the most beautiful lodges in America's national parks. Its granite facade, stained-glass windows, and beamed ceilings are as grand as ever. Enjoy the Native American décor, the gift shop that sells the hotel's custom china, and the walk-in fireplace in the Great Lounge. Free one-hour historic tours of the hotel's public areas take place three times a week; reservations are required (call 209-372-1426). After the tour, have a cocktail in the lounge or on the patio with its views of Glacier Point, and you may just decide to book a room for your next visit.

One of Yosemite Valley's landmarks, **Glacier Point**, is a breathtaking overlook 3,200 feet above the valley floor. **Half Dome**, miles of Sierra peaks, waterfalls, and the valley spread out before visitors, who may have never felt so small and insignificant. Glacier Point is a long drive from the valley (nearly two hours), but it's well worth the trip. (The road to the point is closed in winter.) Hikers may want to take the Glacier Point tour bus (209-372-4386; www.yosemitepark.com) at

Yosemite Lodge and travel one way to the point, and then descend to the valley on foot along the Four Mile Trail, which is actually 5.2 miles. An alternative is to hike up to Glacier Point from the valley floor and take the bus back, a strenuous climb. Hikers should purchase tickets in advance at the lodge tour desk or by calling the number above. Bring lots of water and a camera to capture the awesome scenery along the switchbacks.

The easier, also stunning hike to **Sentinel Dome** is only 1.2 miles long and has an elevation gain of

El Capitan
COURTESY OF YOSEMITE RESORTS

only 450 feet. The trailhead is on Glacier Point Road, about 2 miles before the overlook. (Follow the road sign for TAFT POINT/SENTINEL DOME.) The trail takes walkers to the top of Sentinel for views of Yosemite Falls and the rest of the park.

At the southern entrance of the park, on CA 41 is **Wawona** (see "Where to Sleep"), which was the main trail for Native Americans, early pioneers, and stagecoaches heading to what is now the park. The 1879 **Wawona Hotel** was built for the early tourists; among its guests were President Theodore Roosevelt, who called the park "the most beautiful place in the world." An easy hike, a 3½-mile **Meadow Loop**, starts near the hotel. You can also walk 6 miles (one way) to the **Mariposa Grove of Giant Sequoias** and take a free shuttle bus back to the hotel. Sequoias are some of the largest trees on earth, and 500 of them stand in the grove. A tram tour of the grove is available, or you can walk the 7-mile path that winds through it. You don't have to do the entire hike to see the most incredible of the trees. The largest, the amazing Grizzly Giant, estimated to be between 1,800 and 2,700 years old, is within a mile of the trailhead.

For a High Sierra experience,

take Tioga Road/CA 120 from Yosemite Valley to the park's **Tuolumne Meadows**. There, at 8,775 feet, you can escape the summer crowds; summer is actually the only time to see the area, because Tioga Road is closed in winter. You can either drive the 60 miles (one way) yourself or take the hikers' bus from Yosemite Lodge (about an hour-and-a-half, one-way trip). Along the way the route passes sapphire-blue **Tenaya Lake**.

Trails from Tuolumne Meadows include an 8-mile round-trip John Muir Trail, which gently wanders through the lush meadows and conifer forests of **Lyell Canyon** along a fork of the Tuolumne River. Or, from the Lembert Dome parking lot, follow the **Glen Aulin Trail** along the fast-moving Tuolumne River as it drops to Glen Aulin; the 11-mile round-trip takes you past granite peaks, numerous waterfalls and cascades, and glorious High Sierra landscape.

▮▮▮▮ WHERE TO EAT

Eating establishments are limited in Yosemite Valley and confined to those operated by the concessionaire, Delaware North. **The Ahwahnee**, of course, is the most elegant of the choices. The filet mignon and the farm-raised trout are popular, and the boysenberry pie with a scoop of vanilla ice cream is a bit of culinary history: it has been on the menu since the hotel opened. The Mountain Room at **Yosemite Lodge at the Falls** has a pleasant atmosphere, a view of Yosemite Falls, and straightforward fare such as steaks and pasta. The lodge's food court serves cafeteria-style breakfast, lunch, and dinner. **Curry Village** has similar cafeteria-style dining. In Yosemite Village, the **Village Store** is stocked with fresh fruit and picnic supplies.

▮▮▮▮ WHERE TO SLEEP

Lodging in Yosemite National Park, operated by Delaware North Companies (559-253-5635; www .yosemitepark.com), ranges from canvas tent cabins to the Ahwahnee. **Yosemite Lodge at the Falls** is the best value in the valley. It's worth the extra dollars to upgrade to one of the lodge rooms, which are slightly larger than the hotel's standard rooms and have patios or balconies. Of course, you can always live large and experience the grandeur of the **Ahwahnee**, where the classy rooms, decorated with Native American motifs, start at $426. It requires months-in-advance planning for peak season; in shoulder seasons, it's possible to snag even a last-minute reservation.

Outside of the valley, at the Victorian-era **Wawona Hotel**, you can engage in some old-fashioned lounging on a covered porch and have drinks by the lobby fireplace while listening to a pianist or guitarist. About half of the rooms have shared baths; none have phones or TVs, and there's no cell-phone reception in the area. (The hotel offers a pay phone.) Rooms are decorated with antiques or period reproduction furniture. The hotel has a restaurant, cocktail lounge, and grocery store.

The **Tuolumne Meadows Lodge**, open early June through mid-September, offers simple canvas tents with no electricity. (Candles are provided, and there are wood stoves for heat.) But the lodge is a wonderful base for incredible hiking in the high country. A dining tent serves three family-style meals a day. Make reservations months ahead.

On CA 140 at the El Portal entrance to the park is the resort-like **Yosemite View Lodge** (209-742-7106, 888-742-4371; www .yosemiteresorts.us). Most rooms overlooking the Merced River have balconies and patios. There's an indoor swimming pool and three more pools outside.

You don't need to drive into the valley from here; YARTS (Yosemite Area Regional Transportation System) buses stop regularly (877-989-2787; www.yarts.com) and drop off and pick up at several points in Yosemite Valley.

▮▮▮▮ LOCAL CONTACT

The National Park Service, visitors center in Yosemite Village, 209-372-0200; www.nps.gov /yose.

22 · LAKE TAHOE'S WEST SHORE

Lake Tahoe's north shore gateway, Tahoe City, is about 200 miles from San Francisco. Follow the directions to Sacramento (chapter 16), continuing on I-80 to Truckee. Take CA 89 to Tahoe City. Lake Tahoe's south shore gateway, South Lake Tahoe, is about 180 miles from San Francisco. Follow directions to Sacramento and continue on I-50. Once at the south shore, turn left on CA 89 north.

Of the all places to experience **Lake Tahoe**—the casinos, the ski resorts, the campgrounds, the high mountain trails—the relaxed west shore offers a glimpse into the vacation grandeur of the early 20th century, when the lake was an exclusive playground for wealthy San Franciscans.

Still relatively undeveloped south of Tahoe City, this west, or California, side of the lake is dotted with mansions and lodges built in the "Old Tahoe" style of exposed wood and local stone. These homes are clustered in the small resort communities of Tahoe Pines, Homewood, and Tahoma, and their sandy beaches and marinas look out on glistening deep blue water and the distant Nevada shore.

The 22-mile long lake, ringed by pine forests and snow-capped mountains, is about 1,600 feet deep, making it one of the 10 deepest in the world and perhaps the clearest. The most stunning

example of this clarity on the west shore can be found at **Rubicon Point**, where you can peer 70 feet into water that is gin clear, as martini-loving San Franciscans would say.

To get a sense of Old Tahoe summers, start 10 miles south of Tahoe City on CA 89, at the lake's largest state park, **Sugar Pine Point** (530-525-7982; www.parks .ca.gov). The park encompasses 2,300 acres of sugar pine, fir, aspen, and juniper trees and a 2-mile frontage of the shore. The focal point is **Pine Lodge**, also known as the Ehrman Mansion. It was one of the grand homes built in the early 1900s, a period when San Franciscans packed steamer trunks and boarded trains to take them to the lake's steamboats, which brought them to their houses and resorts. Daily tours during the summer months peek into the mansion's five bedrooms, each of which has call buttons for servants; the dining

Outflow of Lake Tahoe at the Truckee River

The Cedar House Sport Hotel, Truckee

room, where formal evening dress was de rigueur; the big kitchen; and the not-so-big servants' quarters. Every winter, ice was cut into blocks, packed in sawdust, and stored for summer use, because Florence Ehrman, who ran the home for her banker father, believed that fresh ice was tasty and healthy. The mansion's lawns and small beach are lovely picnic spots. The nearby boathouses are part of a Lake Tahoe wood-powerboat tradition that continues today. An example of these boats can be seen in the north boathouse, where the elegant, 26-foot *Cherokee* looks ready to charge.

All along Lake Tahoe's meadows and trails, wildflowers bloom in summer: Indian paintbrush, lupine, columbine, California poppy, Shasta daisy, and more. There are many beautiful hiking trails, but the **Rubicon Trail** is the real showstopper. Pick up a map at **D. L. Bliss State Park**'s visitors center (530-525-7277; www.parks.ca.gov), which itself

is worth a look for its old photos and more than 30 mounted examples of area wildlife—beavers, bobcats, black bears, and all kinds of birds. From the trailhead at Calawee Cove, the path follows the granite-lined shore and crosses Rubicon Point amid a rocky landscape of pines, firs, and cedars. It then extends through 4.6 miles of gorgeous scenery and into dramatic, glacier-carved **Emerald Bay State Park** (530-541-3030; www.parks.ca.gov) and the timbered grandeur of Vikingsholm. Go early in the morning to avoid the crowds along the trail and at Vikingsholm. Organize a car shuttle at Emerald Bay if a one-way hike is all you're after.

D. L. Bliss also features the **Balancing Rock**, 130 tons of granite perched on a slender cone base and a Lake Tahoe attraction for more than a century. It is the highlight of a ½-mile, self-guided nature trail with 19 markers.

From Emerald Bay's Harvey West parking lot and overlook there are stunning views of the turquoise cove with wooded Fannette Island in its center. From the overlook you can head down a mile of steep trail to **Vikingsholm** (530-525-3345; www .vikingsholm.com), one of Lake Tahoe's most photographed sites. The castlelike mansion's traditional Scandinavian architecture shows in its carvings and hand-hewn timbers. The 38-room manor is open for tours from mid-June through September.

Across CA 89 from the Emerald Bay parking lot is the trailhead to **Eagle Falls**, the only waterfall that flows directly into Lake Tahoe. The much-traveled mile hike to Eagle Lake is a steep, heart-pumping trek that affords views of Emerald Bay and beyond. For a more remote and less-visited wilderness experience, continue up the Velma Lakes Trail into Desolation Wilderness to the three Velma lakes; this 9-mile round-trip makes for a strenuous but awesome hike.

The west side of Lake Tahoe has paved, easy bike paths, including one that starts on the south shore and one that starts on the north. (They are not linked for several miles, however.) The **West Shore Bike Trail** on the north end parallels most of CA 89 from Tahoe City to Sugar Pine Point. Bike rentals are available at **West Shore Sports** in Homewood (5395 West Lake Blvd.; 530-525-9920; www.westshoresports.com). From the store, it's a 7-mile round-trip to Sugar Pine.

A lovely longer ride is from Homewood north to Tahoe City, then taking a left at Fanny Bridge and following the bike trail along the **Truckee River**, the only outflow from Lake Tahoe. For a 20-mile round-trip, turn around at River Ranch, whose deck by the rushing water makes a scenic lunch spot. Or continue another 4 miles to **Squaw Valley** ski resort, site of the 1960 Winter Olympic Games.

The resort offers plenty of activities in summer. Its main cable car (530-583-6985; www .squaw.com), open mid-June through mid-September, carries visitors to 8,200-foot High Camp for panoramic views of the lake and the Sierra Nevada. The facility has a spa, a swimming pool "lagoon" with waterfalls and islands, an ice-skating rink, and a restaurant and bar. Tickets are available for the cable car ride only or a combination of the cable car plus swimming and/or ice skating. Try timing the cable car ride for sunset, when the alpenglow lights up the scene.

Another fun option on the Truckee River is a leisurely float trip on a raft from Fanny Bridge to River Ranch, an activity that attracts hundreds on summer weekends. The rafts turn into bumper cars on the 5-mile, gentle-flowing river that follows a stretch of meadows and forested hillsides along the highway. At the bridge, **Truckee River Rafting** (530-583-7238; www.tahoe truckeerafting.com) offers rafts, life jackets, paddles, and a bus ride back to Tahoe City. Look for the company's discount coupons in free local newspapers.

On the south end of the west shore, on CA 89 at Camp Richardson, **Mountain Sports Center** (530-542-6582) rents bikes for the path that parallels the highway for several miles, running through lovely forests almost to Emerald Bay.

Along this stretch is another grand Tahoe summer compound of San Francisco's social elite, **Tallac Historic Site** (530-544-7383; www.tahoeheritage.org), which comprises several lavish individual estates. Art and crafts are for sale at the **Heller Estate**, known as Valhalla, which includes a renovated boathouse and renovated cabins. Other buildings include the handsome 1894 **Pope Estate**, with its large porches and massive fireplaces, and the **Baldwin Estate**, a 4,000-square-foot home built of local logs and housing a museum.

Guided tours, sometimes led by volunteers in clothing of the 1920s, Tallac's heyday, are offered during the summer months.

Just to the north of Tallac, also along the bike trail, is the U.S. Forest Service's **Taylor Creek Visitor Center** (530-543-2674; www .fs.fed.us). The center has picnic areas, nature trails, and an underground viewing area where crayfish and waterfowl can be seen.

The marina at Camp Richardson rents motorboats for waterskiing and fishing, as well as kayaks and canoes. An unforgettable paddling trip is into Emerald Bay, where kayakers can pull up at the boat camp (contact Emerald Bay State Park) to spend the night under the stars. Also along the West Shore, the **High Sierra Water Ski School** (www .highsierrawaterskiing.com) has two marina locations, one at Sunnyside (530-583-7417) and the other at Homewood (530-525-1214). The school offers ski instruction and rents motorboats, Jet Skis, canoes, and kayaks.

▪▪▪▪ WHERE TO EAT

When hunger strikes, there are plenty of west-shore options. At the **Bridgetender Tavern and Grill** in Tahoe City (65 W. Lake Blvd.; 530-583-3342), you can kick back on a deck by the Truckee River and have a beer and grilled hamburger. **Fire Sign Cafe** (1785 W. Lake Blvd.; 530-583-0871) is a local favorite for breakfast and lunch. Customers begin lining up at 7 AM for made-from-scratch coffee cake, smoked salmon, egg scrambles, and huevos rancheros. Pick up picnic supplies at **Tahoe House** (625 W. Lake Blvd.; 530-583-1377; www.tahoe-house.com), a European-style bakery and cafe where sandwiches are made from delicious fresh-baked bread. **Sunnyside** (1850 W. Lake Blvd.; 530-583-7200; www.sunnysideresort.com) is a popular bar and restaurant where boaters pull up at the dock for cocktails and a menu big on steaks and seafood. The newcomer and most upscale dining option is the **West Shore Cafe** (5160 W. Lake Blvd.; 530-525-5200; www.westshorecafe.com), an elegant restaurant with an outdoor cocktail lounge on a pier heated by overhead lamps—a spine-tingling setting at sunset.

At Camp Richardson, the **Beacon Bar and Grill** (530-541-0631; www.camprichardson.com) is a casual restaurant known for its clam chowder. The large lakeside deck by the long sandy beach gets lively when bands play in the summer (from 2 to 6 PM) and customers enjoy the bar's Rum Runner cocktail.

▪▪▪▪ WHERE TO SLEEP

Tahoma Meadows Cottages (6821 W. Lake Blvd.; 530-525-1553, 866-525-1553; www.tahoma meadows.com) attracts a loyal clientele, and it's easy to see why: its cheery cottages have claw-foot soaking tubs, fireplaces, and decks with private gardens. The Alpen Glow cottage is especially homey. Four cottages have kitchens. Guests get a discount on bike rentals at West Shore Sports. The **Cottage Inn** (1690 W. Lake Blvd.; 530-581-4073, 800-581-4073; www.the cottageinn.com) is an authentic Old Tahoe lodge and one of the most romantic in the area. The fairytale cottages, built with knotty pine paneling in 1938, have been remodeled with modern baths. Each has a fireplace, TV, and sitting area with a view through the pine forest to the inn's private beach. The Enchanted Cottage has whirlpool tub by a fireplace.

Chaney House (4725 W. Lake Blvd.; 530-525-7333; www.chaney house.com) doesn't just feel like a warm family home—it is one. The innkeepers, Gary and Lori Chaney, raised their children here. The home's thick stone walls and huge fireplace of local river rock were built by an Italian craftsman in the 1920s. The house has its own private pier and beach. The Russell Suite is a charming hideaway up a circular staircase. For more privacy, ask for the honeymoon suite in the guest cottage.

Just outside the town of Truckee is the **Cedar House Sport Hotel** (10918 Brockway Rd.; 866-582-5655; www.cedarhousesporthotel .com), a European-style lodge that exudes cool. Modern architecture, environmentally friendly building techniques, and stylish rooms set the scene for a hip experience warmed by the presence of owner Patricia Baird, who greets guests in the cafelike lobby. Even the standard rooms have fluffy down comforters, luxurious linens, and flat-screen TVs.

▮▮▮▮ LOCAL CONTACT

Lake Tahoe Visitors Authority (for south shore), 775-588-5900, www.bluelaketahoe.com. **North Lake Tahoe Visitors and Convention Bureau**, visitors center at 380 N. Lake Blvd., Tahoe City, 530-581-8703, 800-462-5196, www.gotahoe.north.com.

23 • LAKES BASIN

The Lakes Basin area is about 260 miles from San Francisco and 170 miles from Sacramento. From Truckee (see chapter 22) take CA 89 north through Sierraville and turn onto the Gold Lake Road.

A stay in the **Lakes Basin** is a trip back in time to when the pace of life was slower and Americans took long summer vacations. Families still typically spend a week or more here. However, one- and two-night getaways are possible because many of the old lodges no longer require seven-night bookings.

The region is a hidden treasure that even native Northern Californians have trouble locating on a map. You might hear, "Just turn left at Truckee," the old railroad town on I-80 that is the northern gateway to Lake Tahoe. When you turn west on CA 89 at Truckee (instead of east toward Tahoe), you enter a rural landscape, where weathered old barns seem to outnumber people—a place far removed from the casinos, strips of motels, and congestion of the Tahoe Basin.

Driving 50 miles west of Truckee brings you to **Graeagle**, an old lumber-mill town where all the buildings are painted the same shade of deep red. Today, Graea-

gle is a quiet, golf-oriented resort that is slowly gaining more attention, as the addition of more courses has turned it into a popular destination for in-the-know duffers. Nearby **Whitehawk** is ranked as one of the top 12 public courses in California.

Still, the region seems as wild as when mountain man James P. Beckwourth, an African American, discovered the lowest pass across the Sierra Nevada in 1850, creating a wagon trail for emigrants from western Nevada through Plumas County to Sacramento.

A highlight is the **Lakes Basin Recreation Area** (530-836-2575; www.fs.fed.us), a vast region dotted with numerous trout-filled alpine lakes. People may argue which lake is the most beautiful, but most will end up agreeing it is Sardine Lake, with its postcard-perfect setting at the base of the craggy Sierra Buttes. The lodge at Sardine is difficult to book (see "Where to Sleep"), but you can still enjoy the lake and the restaurant (see "Where to Eat") and make it a picnic and hiking spot. There's an easy, 2½-mile round-trip walk from the lodge parking lot to Upper Sardine Lake, an ideal place for a picnic lunch or an afternoon of enjoying the views. For riding through the basin's grassy meadows and pine forests, stables rent horses for one hour and longer (530-836-0430; www.reidhorse.com).

Rising high above the Lakes Basin landscape are the **Sierra Buttes**, jagged peaks capped by snow, often through the summer. On the highest is a lookout reached via 176-step aluminum stairways that seem suspended in midair. As the song says, "On a clear day, you can see forever"— or at least to the Tahoe Basin and distant Mount Lassen and Mount Shasta. You can drive up to the lookout, but only with a four-wheel-drive vehicle; the steep, narrow road from Packer Lake to the lot is about ¾ mile from the staircase. Or you can hike up on a moderately difficult, 3-mile trek with two steep switchback sec-

tions; the trailhead is up the road from Packer Lake about 4 miles. The elevation gain is about 1,500 feet, starting at 7,000 and rising to 8,587 feet at the tower.

One of the easiest and most beautiful Lakes Basin hikes is the **Round Lake Trail**, a 3¾-mile walk that takes a little over two hours and has little elevation gain. To get to the trailhead, drive about 5 miles from Graeagle on the Gold Lake Road until you see the sign for Round Lake Trail; the parking area is on the left. Much of the trail is an old wagon road. You'll pass an old mine and see views of glacial lakes everywhere on this loop route. Wildflowers put on a show from June through August.

An even easier and shorter hike is to **Frazier Falls**; the gentle, paved trail is only ½ mile from the overlook above the 250-foot falls. The trailhead is on the Gold Lake Road, about 6 miles from the CA 89/Gold Lake Road intersection. The overlook is a good place for a picnic, and it has restrooms.

The Sierra Buttes tower over the Lakes Basin.

The Lodge at Whitehawk

WHERE TO EAT

For breakfast or lunch, try the **Bonta Street Bistro** (190 Bonta St.; 530-836-1497), a darling log cabin in Blairsden near Graeagle. They make delicious French toast. For lunch, grilled panini sandwiches are the specialty. Also in Blairsden, an old wooden building houses the **Grizzly Grill** (250 Bonta St., 530-836-1300), which serves pastas, fish, steak, and other dishes more sophisticated than you'd think you'd find here. For dinner, check out **Sardine Lake Resort** (990 Sardine Lake Rd.; 530-862-1196), a real old-fashioned, meat-and-potatoes sort of place; chops and prime rib dominate the menu. With those incredible views of the lake and the Buttes beyond, no wonder people cling to their yearly cabin reservations. Several more restaurants can be found in Sierra City (see chapter 20), about a half hour away from Graeagle.

WHERE TO SLEEP

Many of the old lodges tucked away in the basin—such as Packer Lake Lodge and Sardine Lake Resort, with their stunning lakeside settings—are nearly impossible to book. As one local put it, a reservation is more difficult to snag than tickets on the 50-yard line for a Forty-Niners game.

Families come annually and reserve for the following year as soon as the books open. These lodges also have short seasons, typically from May through October, although the seasons can vary according to snowfall.

Two establishments, however, are easier to book, probably because they don't have a lakeside setting; however, both are still within easy walking distance of the lakes. **Gray Eagle Lodge** (5000 Gold Lake Rd.; 800-635-8778; www.grayeaglelodge.com) is a hiker's paradise set in the middle of Lakes Basin and has been run by the same family since 1923. A stay here at this rustic but civilized lodge includes breakfast and dinner. A full bar offers cocktails before dinner, and afterwards guests can gather next to the big, stone fireplace in the cozy living room. There are no TVs at Gray Eagle, but the fireplace indoors and campfires outdoors make for much better entertainment than any television show. During the day, you can use the rowboat that the lodge keeps docked at nearby Smith Lake. All of the cabins have private baths. The two-person Poplar Cabin is right on the river and has a nice deck overlooked by a towering fir tree.

Gold Lake Lodge (7000 Gold Lake Rd.; 530-836-2350; www

.goldlakelodge.com) has just 10 spare but comfortable cabins in a forest meadow. The price of a stay covers three hearty, mountain-appetite-sized meals that are served at communal tables in the charming pine-paneled dining room. Lunch fixings are put out in the mornings, and dinners offer a choice of 14 entrees. A rowboat for guests' exclusive use is docked at Big Bear Lake, a short walk away; three other boats are available at Long Lake.

For more luxury and modernity, go just outside Lakes Basin to **Chalet View** (72056 Hwy. 70, 5 miles east of Graeagle , 800-510-8439, www.chaletviewlodge .com), which opened in 2002. Designed with lofts and slate floors, decorated with antiques, and furnished with flat-screen TVs, the rooms are quite agreeable, though the ones facing the highway get a little road noise.

Chalet View also has nice pool area and a patio for breakfast and evening cocktails.

Also built in recent years is the **Lodge at Whitehawk** (985 Whitehawk Dr., Clio, 530-836-4985, 877-945-6343; www.lodgeat whitehawk.com), which features a tennis court, a trout pond, and access to the community pool. It offers 14 cabins with decks and wooden floors and paneling. Guests get a discount at the spectacular Whitehawk golf course next door. The lodge's restaurant serves breakfast and dinner. Book far in advance for summer weekends.

▋▋▋▋ LOCAL CONTACT

Eastern Plumas County Chamber of Commerce, visitors center at corner of State Route 70 and CA 89 in Blairsden, 530-836-6811; 800-995-6057, www.eastern plumaschamber.com.

HEADING SOUTH:

Within 100 Miles of San Francisco

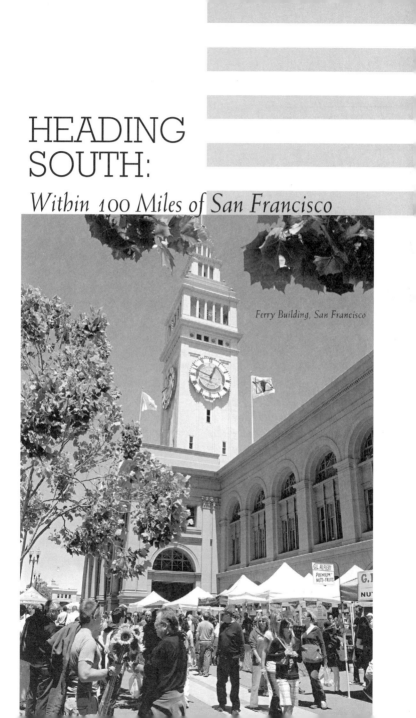

Ferry Building, San Francisco

24 • SAN FRANCISCO: THE EMBARCADERO

The Embarcadero and the Ferry Building are easily accessible by public transportation, including ferry from Marin and Alameda counties. The Bay Area Rapid Transit (BART) and the San Francisco Municipal Railway (better known as the Muni) Metro both stop at the Embarcadero station.

Shocking as it may seem, San Francisco's planners once set out to encircle their beautiful city with freeways. The first section of that system, the Embarcadero Freeway, effectively cut off the waterfront from the rest of the city. A local journalist called it a "double-decker prison wall." It was so disliked that the envisioned Los Angeles—type maze of concrete went no further, but for a quarter century, the wharves and piers, the warehouses and the Ferry Building, seemed isolated in the shadow and noise of the viaduct overhead.

Then came the Loma Prieta earthquake.

The quake of October 1989 did some of its worst damage to 1950s-vintage double freeways. Among others, the Embarcadero Freeway had to be torn down. Almost overnight, an obscured area became full of possibilities.

Since the late 1990s, redevelopment has transformed **the Embarcadero**, creating a wide, palm tree-lined boulevard. New plazas, parks, promenades, and public piers continue to spring up. The past isn't forgotten: bronze plaques in the boulevard's middle plaza mark spots where the freeway's pillars once stood. A prominent feature along the Embarcadero is the F-line streetcar, a link of the municipal railway that runs vintage streetcars, some quite colorful, from around the world. From the Castro District, the streetcars roll down Market Street and then rumble up the Embarcadero to Fisherman's Wharf.

The redevelopment's focal point is the 1898 **Ferry Building**, once the busiest transportation hub in the world. It withstood the Loma Prieta upheaval, as it did the 1906 earthquake and fire, when thousands fled the burning city from its docks. The building's resiliency is due to its strong yet flexible foundation:

reinforced concrete supported on pilings of five thousand Oregon pine trees. Neglected for decades as water transportation dwindled, the Ferry Building was reborn in the late 1990s as a culinary mecca—a one-stop shop for the best in Northern California food—and a destination for connoisseurs or anyone with an interest in good eats.

The Ferry Building is worth a wander any time, but try to visit on one of the farmers' market days (Tuesday from 10 AM to 2 PM, Thursday from 3 to 7 PM, Saturday from 8 AM to 2 PM, and Sunday from 9 AM to 3 PM) when rows of stands sell a dazzling array of fruit, vegetables, and locally made products (see "Where to Eat"). At the permanent shops, you can collect supplies for a classic picnic on the pier: a loaf of bread at Acme bakery, a cheese wedge from Cowgirl Creamery (try its award-winning Humboldt Fog or the St. Pat, a soft, mellow cow's cheese), and a bottle of wine from the Ferry Building Wine Merchant. Then choose some fresh fruit from Capay or Frog Hollow and a French pastry at Miette—and *voilà*!

To understand the critical role the waterfront played in San Francisco history, **City Guides** (415-557-4266; www.sfcityguides .org), a San Francisco volunteer organization, offers a 45-minute Ferry Building stroll each Saturday at noon, starting at the main entrance near the stairs. Two other City Guides tours dig deeper in waterfront history. The Embarcadero North walk, on the second Saturday of each month, covers of the rise and fall of the port, the dockworkers' strike that rocked the city in the 1930s, and the waterfront's role in World War II. For those shipping out to Europe and the South Pacific, San Francisco was usually the last look at the U.S.A.; for those on leave and liberty, Frisco, as they called it, was the town for R&R— and it still is. The Embarcadero South walk, conducted on the fourth Saturday of each month, takes in the history of the Rincon area south of Market Street—San Francisco's first fashionable neighborhood—and the Bay Bridge.

The promenade along the waterfront is commonly called the Embarcadero but was renamed **Herb Caen Way** after the late *San Francisco Chronicle* columnist, whose work was featured daily from the late 1930s to 1997. Though he lambasted the Embarcadero Freeway (and other edifices and individuals he did not care for), excerpts from his columns, inscribed on historic markers along the waterfront, are love notes to the city he found endlessly fascinating.

Directly across the Embarcadero from the Ferry Building is **Justin Herman Plaza**, a four-acre open space that bustles at lunchtime with free concerts and rows of craftspeople selling their creations. On one side is Vaillancourt Fountain, a mass of concrete in various shapes, much of it resembling aluminum-foil cartons. Some call it art; others (like Herb Caen) have referred to it in terms less kind.

The **Hyatt Regency San Francisco** towers over the scene. Take a peek inside the lobby for its architecture: it was one of the first hotels to be built with an atrium. The glass-enclosed elevators that travel up and down the atrium's 17 stories can be seen in the Mel Brooks film *High Anxiety* and Irwin Allen's *The Towering Inferno*. (The latter movie, according to Herb Caen, contained two things you'll never see in San Francisco: fire engines racing down Market Street side by side and citizens cheering the mayor.)

To the north of the Ferry Building is a new promenade, starting along **Pier 1**, with photo displays and markers describing the city's maritime history. The old ferryboat *Santa Rosa*, tied up along the walkway at **Pier 3**, is an example of the car ferries that served San Francisco before the bridges were built in the 1930s. From here, the promenade links to **Pier 7**, a pretty, Victorian-style jetty lined with benches and old fashioned lamps; it offers marvelous views of the city, particularly at night.

Walking south from the Ferry Building, you'll encounter sculptures such as Claes Oldenburg's *Cupid's Span*, a 60-foot-tall bow and arrow rising out of two-acre **Rincon Park**. **Pier 14**, which juts out from the park, is a good place to gaze at the city's waterfront and the Bay Bridge. Take a twirl on one of the steel seats (they spin) and watch tugboats, freighters, sailboats, motorboats, rowboats, and kayaks glide by.

Cross the boulevard and walk a block up Spear Street between Mission and Market and enter **One Market Plaza**, the historic Southern Pacific building. Take one of the elevators to the seventh floor, and you'll find one of San Francisco's hidden rooftop gardens, offering one of the best views of the waterfront from a public space.

Walking further south along the Embarcadero toward the Bay Bridge, you'll see plenty of cranes, evidence of an area in transition from maritime industry to office buildings and luxury condominiums. But relics from earlier eras remain: the San Francisco Fire Department's 1915 boathouse at Pier 22½, where *Phoenix* (the fireboat that saved the marina in 1989) and *Guardian* are docked; Red's Java House, a classic old beanery perched on Pier 30; and, farther south, the just-plain Java House, which is packed with Giants fans before and after games.

You can end your Embarcadero wanderings on its southern end. There San Francisco's newest neighborhood, South Beach, is rising around red-brick AT&T Park, the home of the San Francisco Giants.

Other ballparks have debuted since **AT&T Park** (24 Willie Mays Plaza; 415-972-2400; www.att park.com) opened in 2000, but this one is still considered the most impressive. You can walk along the bay channel where the occasional "splash hit" falls, and, if it's a game day, peek in the park's fence, where you're allowed to watch the game free of charge for a few minutes. If it's not game day, consider the hour-and-a-half tours. They feature visits to the dugouts, the warming track, and luxury suites. The tours are conducted daily at 10:30 AM and 12:30 PM and involve about 2 miles of walking through the vast stadium.

The flat, wide Embarcadero makes a good bike trail, although there is city traffic to contend with. Many cyclists find it a fun urban adventure. Rent a bike south of the Bay Bridge at **Bike Hut** (Pier 40, 415-543-4335; www .thebikehut.com), a nonprofit that trains local low-income kids in cycle mechanics. **Blazing Saddles** (five locations on the waterfront; 415-202-8888; www.blazing saddles.com) has a bigger fleet

The Harbor Court Hotel and San Francisco skyline from Pier 14

Saturday morning at the farmers' market

and provides maps for self-guided tours. The more ambitious (and those who have three to four hours to spare) may want to keep riding along the Embarcadero north, past Fisherman's Wharf and Aquatic Park, through Presidio National Park's Crissy Field, up and over the Golden Gate Bridge, and down to Sausalito, then return by ferry to Fisherman's Wharf or the Ferry Building. This bike ride has become a San Francisco classic.

▪▪▪▪ WHERE TO EAT

On Saturday mornings, not only do some of the top food producers of Northern California offer their fruit, vegetables, and other wares at the Ferry Building, but restaurants also set up temporary shop in the plaza outside, selling takeaway breakfast and lunch. The lines can be long, and you'll end up juggling paper plates and drinks while you scramble to find a place at the picnic tables facing the Bay Bridge, but regulars love it. "Coming here on Saturday mornings is like going to church for me," one woman confided. Some of the favorite stands are those from the **Hayes Street Grill**, which has a dreamy scrambled eggs dish with either bacon or wild mushrooms. **Primavera** serves mouth-watering Mexican fare, including huevos rancheros and chilaquiles with eggs and avocados.

Among the noteworthy restaurants inside the Ferry Building are the **Slanted Door** (415-861-8032; www.slanteddoor.com), known for innovative Vietnamese dishes served in a sleek atmosphere overlooking the bay, and two casual lunch spots: **Hog Island Oyster Company** (415-391-7117; www.hogislandoysters.com), where you can sit at the u-shaped oyster bar for fresh-shucked oysters and clam chowder, and **Mijita** (415-399-0814; www.mijitasf .com), which dishes out superb regional Mexican dishes, such as Oaxacan chicken tamales. Or enjoy San Francisco classics— shrimp Louis or crab Louis—with a local Anchor Steam beer at **Ferry Plaza Seafood**'s marble counters, which face picture windows overlooking the docks.

Steuart Street, one block east of the Embarcadero between Mission and Howard, is lined with fine restaurants, including one of the city's top spots for Japanese food, **Ozumo** (161 Steuart; 415-882-1333; www.ozumo.com). Also on Steuart is **Shanghai 1930** (133 Steuart; 415-896-5600; www .shanghai1930.com), an elegant Chinese restaurant and sultry, film-noir lounge with live jazz music each night.

▌▌▌▌ WHERE TO SLEEP

When it opened in 2005, **Hotel Vitale** (8 Mission St.; 415-278-3700, 888-890-8688; www.hotel vitale.com) captured the buzz as the place to stay in San Francisco. The sleek interior uses rich, natural materials to create a feeling of serenity. The knockout rooms are the waterfront suites with 180-degree views of the bay and two-person limestone soaking tubs. Don't miss the landscaped rooftop terraces with bridge views. Sunday night stays are the best value. The hotel's Americano restaurant and bar attracts a young after-work crowd, which gathers in the outdoor lounge warmed by heaters on San Francisco's chilly evenings.

From the eclectic, modern décor in the recently renovated rooms, now with flat-panel TVs, you'd never guess the **Harbor Court** (165 Steuart St.; 415-882-1300; www.harborcourthotel.com) is in a historic building. The bayfront hotel, which has a YMCA (including one of the city's few indoor pools) that guests can access, remains one of the city's best values, considering the views from the waterfront rooms. Try to land one of the "hot dates" deals that often pop up on the hotel's Web site.

The **Orchard Garden Hotel** (466 Bush St.; 415-399-9007; www .theorchardgardenhotel.com) is San Francisco's first "green" hotel, built from the ground up with in-room recycling systems. It is several blocks from the Embarcadero, near Union Square. Rooms are decorated in a restful minimalist style and, appropriately, a nature motif. Interior rooms have excellent rates. They don't have much natural light, but that's fine if you're planning to be out and about.

▌▌▌▌ LOCAL CONTACT

San Francisco Convention and Visitors Bureau, visitors center at 900 Market St., 415-391-2000, www.onlyinsanfrancisco.com.

25 • SAN FRANCISCO: THE MISSION DISTRICT

The Mission District is well served by public transportation from other parts of San Francisco and the entire Bay Area. Bay Area Rapid Transit (BART) has two stops (at 16th and 24th streets). The San Francisco Municipal Railway (Muni) bus and streetcar lines (the 14-Mission and J-Church are the main ones) connect it to downtown San Francisco.

The Mission District is the city's most vibrant neighborhood, and its residents reflect its layers of history: tatooed artists and hipsters, political activists, gays and lesbians, Latino immigrants, young professionals, and original San Franciscans interact in an environment that is sunny, history rich, sometimes seedy, and always urban and cutting edge.

The Mission was a working-class area until the late 20th century, with a concentration of Irish and Italians and, later, Latinos. When the mid-1990s dot-com boom brought droves of young high-tech workers to San Francisco, many settled in the Mission District, giving it new energy (and higher real estate prices).

Blocks of the Mission District, particularly along Mission Street between 14th and 25th streets, are lined with Mexican and Central American *taquerias*, repair shops and grocery stores where you'll hear Latin music and TVs tuned to Spanish-language channels. You'll see wandering mariachi bands and popsicle vendors pushing carts, bells ringing.

One block east of Mission, **Valencia** is lined with one-of-a-kind clothing and furniture shopping, alternative bookstores, cafes and restaurants between 16th and 24th streets. Check out **Dema** (1038 Valencia), a 1960s-influenced women's clothing designer; **Modern Times** (888 Valencia), a far-left bookstore; and **the Apartment** (3469 18th St., near Valencia), a vintage furniture showroom. A block east of Valencia, Guerrero, offers a quieter, different scene. Here, along a burgeoning gourmet row at 18th Street, hipsters sip cappuccino and dine on some of the best food in California. This area at Guerrero and 18th also includes a sweet baby clothes and gift shop, **Stem** (3690 18th St.).

Because of San Francisco's peculiar microclimates, the Mission sunbelt can be 10 degrees warmer in the summers than in Golden Gate Park and at the ocean beaches on the other side of town. On sunny days, **Dolores Park**, bordered by 18th and 20th streets and shaded by palm trees, is full of bathing-suit-clad loungers enjoying scheduled events: an opera or symphony performance, a Latin festival, a play or a political demonstration.

To get a grasp of the area's early history, start at the adobe-built **Mission Dolores** (321 16th St.; 415-621-8302; www.mission dolores.org). Established in 1776, it is the oldest building in San Francisco and the oldest church in California. Its beautiful patch-work-painted beamed ceiling resembles the basket weaving of local Native Americans. A grave-yard with markers dating from 1830 is surrounded by gardens restored to the way they were in 1791.

If you're visiting on a Sunday, check out the tour by **City Guides** (415-557-4266; www.sfcityguides .com), a local volunteer organization, which conducts free Mission Dolores neighborhood walks year round, on Sunday at noon. Walks start at 20th Street and Dolores, at the golden fire hydrant at the top of Dolores Park. Here,

in 1906, as the fire that erupted after the earthquake headed westward from downtown, firefighters made a stand, as water gushed from this hydrant when others failed. Thousands left homeless by the disaster congregated in Dolores Park and lived there for months in one-room "earthquake shacks." The two-hour tour traces the fire line along 20th Street, where the fire was stopped. The results are still dramatic: on the south side of 20th Street are Victorians dating from the 1870s; on the north side, the buildings were all built after 1906.

Ever wondered about the architectural differences between Italianate Victorian, Queen Anne, and Edwardian buildings? They are covered on the tour, which pauses throughout the **Liberty Street Historic District**. Because of the 1906 quake, San Francisco has thousands of handsome Edwardians: the city's massive rebuilding took place from 1906 to 1910, the Edwardian era. In the mid-20th century, the Victorians and Edwardians were often torn down or radically altered. Not until the late 1960s and 1970s were the ornate old homes appreciated again, giving rise to the city's "painted ladies." (Original Victorian homes, however, were actually duller than today's bright-colored renovated buildings.)

The City Guides walk takes you past two examples of the Mission's many murals: one at the Mission Pool at 19th and Linda streets and one at the Women's Building on 18th Street between Valencia and Guerrero. The latter depicts goddesses and women of significance. All of the Mission's murals are maintained by the **Precita Eyes Mural Center** (415-285-2287; www.precitaeyes.org) at 2981 24th St., where you can stop for a map of the murals and more details about them.

City Guides conducts two other tours in the area: "Mission Murals Tours" (first and third Saturday of the month, 11 AM) and "Murals and Multi-Ethnic Mission" (Sunday, noon).

The Mission, a magnet for the city's activists and artists, is full of nonprofit organizations open for visits. They include **826 Valencia/the Pirate Store** (826 Valencia St.; 415-642-5905; www.826valencia.org), where you can buy message bottles, eye patches, and pirates' blouses to create your own Johnny Depp moment. The store is a "front" for an innovative group that offers tutoring and writing classes to school-age children. Another nonprofit that's open to the public is **Creativity Explored** (3245 16th St.; 415-863-2108; www.creativityexplored.org), where artists with develop-

mental disabilities (some of them previously institutionalized) work in a large studio that doubles as a gallery. The **Mission Cultural Center** (2868 Mission St.; 415-821-1155; www.missionculturalcenter

San Francisco's Mission Dolores

Bi-Rite Market in San Francisco's Mission District

.org) is a community hub, offering drop-in art classes, exhibits, and performances. Check the chalkboard outside for the pies of the day at **Mission Pie** (2901 Mission St.; 415-282-1500; www.pie ranch.org), which hires high school kids to help at its coastal farm and to make pies and fruit-filled pastries in the bakery.

The Mission is a hotbed of not only the culinary scene (see "Where to Eat"), but also of San Francisco avant garde art and theater. Among the small theaters is **Intersection for the Arts** (466 Valencia St.; 415-626-2787; www .theintersection.org), which offers new and experimental works in dance, music, plays, and literature, and **the Marsh** (1062 Valenca St.; 415-826-5750; www.themarsh.org), which showcases the lyrical tales of monologists. **The Roxie** (3117 16th St.; 415-863-1087; www.roxie.com), a cinema that dates from 1909, shows arty films and provocative documentaries.

Nightlife here is thriving with a bar- and club-hopping scene. **Revolution Cafe** (3248 22nd St. at Bartlett; 415-642-6474), a cafe and bar that looks airlifted from a sultry Latin American city, has live music many nights. **Elbo Room** (647 Valencia St.; 415-552-7788; www.elbo.com), a former speakeasy where live bands perform and DJs spin, mixes delicious cocktails during what is billed as San Francisco's longest happy hour—from 5 to 9 PM. Another spot for drinks is **Medjool's Sky Terrace** (2522 Mission St.; 415-550-9055; www.medjool sf.com), which has awesome city views.

▪▪▪▪ WHERE TO EAT

There are hundreds of restaurants in the Mission—no doubt the most varied selection in a city known for its diverse and ethnic fare. Start the day at the **Dolores Park Cafe** (501 Dolores at 18th St.; 415-621-2936), a bustling coffeehouse with scrambled egg breakfasts served all day, or the acclaimed **Tartine Bakery** (600 Guerrero; 487-2600; www.tartine bakery.com), where the brandy-laced frangipane croissant with almonds is unforgettable. The 18th Street block is home to **Delfina** (3621 18th St.; 415-552-4055; www.delfinasf.com) and its pizzeria, one of the city's top Italian restaurants. It is known for the simple, deep flavors of its signature dishes, such as grilled calamari with white bean salad and buttermilk panna cotta with blackberries. Poke around a foodie paradise, **Bi-Rite Market** (3639 18th St.; 415-241-9760; www .biritemarket.com), for picnic supplies to take to Dolores Park.

Although **Bi-Rite Creamery** (3692 18th St.; 415-626-5600; www.biritecreamery.com) is a newcomer, lines form here for its silky homemade ice cream. (Try the brown butter pecan and the salted caramel.)

Dozens of hole-in-the-wall Mexican and Salvadoran eateries line the Mission's streets. Many aficionados swear by cafeteria-style **La Taqueria** (2889 Mission St.; 415-285-7117) for the best tacos in town. The carnitas tacos are the favorite. Colorful, inexpensive **Taqueria Cancun** operates three San Francisco locations, including two in the Mission (2288 Mission St.; 415-252-9560; and 3211 Mission St.; 415-550-2424); all serve burritos, tacos, and *aguas frescas*—Mexican fresh fruit drinks. **Panchita's #3** (3115 22nd St.; 415-821-6660) specializes in the El Salvadoran national dish, *pupusas*: fluffy grilled tortillas oozing with a spicy combination of cheese and meat.

Much more upscale is **Foreign Cinema** (2534 Mission St.; 415-648-7600; www.foreigncinema.com), where dining is memorable. Seductive seared scallops, beef carpaccio, and chocolate pots de creme are served outdoors on the heated patio as classic movies flicker on the back wall. Another example of California cuisine at its best can be found at **Range** (824 Valencia; 415-282-8283; www.rangesf.com). **Dosa** (995 Valencia; 415-642-3672; www.dosasf.com), named after its delicious savory crêpe specialty, is one of the Bay Area's few southern Indian restaurants. If the wait is long and you are craving something from the subcontinent, walk half a block to **Aslam's Rasoi** (1037 Valencia St.; 415-695-0599; www.aslamsrasoi.com) for satisfying Pakistani-Indian dishes, including many vegetarian options.

■ ■ ■ ■ WHERE TO SLEEP

The **Parker Guest House** (520 Church St.; 415-621-3222; www.parkerguesthouse.com) is a combined 1890s Victorian and 1906 Edwardian with many original fixtures, such as stained-glass windows. It has 21 rooms and quiet landscaped grounds. Room 36 is bright, large, and sunny; Room 19 has a travertine marble shower.

Noe's Nest (1257 Guerrero; 415-821-0751; www.noesnest.com) is an 1887 Victorian that was once a brothel and gaming house. (Ask about how the working women secretly moved from room to room.) It has nine flowery, Victorian-style rooms, including seven with private baths. The Cabana Room has its own entrance, kitchenette, and French doors that open to the garden. Three of the rooms have wood-burning fireplaces. If you don't mind stairs, ask for the View Room, which has gorgeous vistas of the city.

If you've wanted to stay in an ornate Victorian mansion, **Inn San Francisco** (943 South Van Ness Ave.; 415-641-0188; www.inn sf.com) is your place. The 135-year-old home is a beautiful example of the period, and it has fireplaces, feather beds, and marble baths. Make you way up the rickety circular staircase to the roof garden for a 360-degree panoramic view. The neighborhood is on the gritty side, but the lovely, lush garden with hot tub makes it seem far away.

▌▌▌▌ LOCAL CONTACT

San Francisco Convention and Visitors Bureau, visitors center at 900 Market St.; 415-391-2000; www.onlyinsanfrancisco.com.

26 • HALF MOON BAY

Half Moon Bay is about 25 miles south of San Francisco on CA1.
Take I-280 south to the Pacifica/CA 1 exit.

Half Moon Bay is within only an hour's drive of big population centers of San Francisco, Oakland, and San Jose, but it has managed to hang on to its small-town character. Only winding two-lane highways connect it to the cities, and growth limits have kept much of the surrounding, often fog-shrouded coastline undeveloped. For a getaway, there is a little of everything: a variety of accommodations, dining, shopping, gorgeous scenery, and many places to explore—particularly miles of public beaches with sandy coves, rocky cliffs, tide pools, and hiking, fishing, and picnic spots.

Half Moon Bay remains a farm and fishing town at heart, even though lots of high-tech industry executives from over the hill in Silicon Valley have moved in. An old-fashioned Main Street is lined with art galleries, bookstores, gift shops, and restaurants. A smattering of older businesses, such as the Cunha Country Store and the Half Moon Bay Feed and Fuel Store (the latter established decades ago to serve the Portuguese and Italians who settled here to fish or grow artichokes) keep the town from falling into preciousness.

Autumn is Half Moon Bay's busiest tourist season. The skies are clear, the coast gets some of its warmest weather, and the surrounding fields are filled with orange pumpkins. The Half Moon Bay Art and Pumpkin Festival, typically held the second weekend of October, draws families, who make it a tradition to travel here to pick out their pumpkins and see the big ones compete in the World Champion Pumpkin Weigh-Off.

Besides pumpkins, the farms spread along the coastline grow artichokes, Brussels sprouts, and some of the most delectable sweet English peas you've ever tasted. Farm stands along CA 1 and stores in Half Moon Bay sell the local produce, and a farmers' market sets up in the parking lot at 845 Main Street on Saturday from 9 AM to 1 PM.

Undoubtedly, the draw of Half Moon Bay is the Pacific Ocean. When you see a brown-and-white

Coastal Access sign along CA 1 pointing down one of the many roads heading west, follow it. You'll hit some beautiful beaches, such as **Half Moon Bay State Beach**, a long, wide, sandy swath where you might spot a sea otter or a dolphin (binoculars help). The lovely Coastal Trail is a nice walk 3 miles north to the hamlet of Miramar along the bluffs. **Sea Horse Ranch and Friendly Acres** (650-726-2362; www.horserentals .com) offers a large stable of horses for individual rentals or trail rides to the beach; no reservations are necessary.

All the area beaches are prime locations from which to watch the annual gray whale migration—when an estimated 15,000 whales swim south from the Arctic to Baja California—from December through May. **The Oceanic Society** (415-474-3385; www.oceanic -society.org) operates three-hour, naturalist-led cruises from the Princeton harbor just north of Half Moon Bay. For an even closer look at the marine life, the **Half Moon Bay Kayak Company** (650-773-6101; www.hmbkayak.com) at the harbor rents kayaks and leads guided tours for beginners and more advanced kayakers. Even if you're not going out on the water, walk around the harbor and onto the piers. In the mornings, you can buy just-

caught crab, bass, salmon, or halibut, depending on the season, right off the fishing boats.

South of Half Moon Bay the landscape gets more rural and the beaches more isolated. The tiny **San Gregorio General Store** (Hwy. 84 at Stage Rd., San Gregorio; 650-726-0565; www.san gregoriostore.com) dates back to 1889. Within the store is an old bar and quirky gift shop with the usual candles-and-refrigerator-magnet selection, but the store also has all the cast-iron skillets, cowboy hats, and anything else you might need to outfit a ranch. On Saturday and Sunday afternoons, the place comes alive with live bluegrass, Irish, and folk music.

From the general store, head south to **Pescadero** by going one of two ways: along CA 1 or by driving the narrow and winding Stage Road; the latter is especially pretty in the spring when the hills are green. Pescadero is a farm town with a few antiques and gift shops and an old-fashioned grocery store, Arcangeli (also known as Norm's), which carries picnic goodies and a famous-in-these-parts artichoke bread. But Pescadero is best known as the home of Duarte's Tavern (see "Where to Eat").

Two miles east from town is the **Phipps Country Store and Farm**

(2700 Pescadero Rd.; 650-879-0787; www.phippscountry.com). The store sells a mind-boggling array of dried beans, fresh produce, and local jam. At the farm, you can pick berries in season. The barnyard area, with its goats, rabbits, ducks, and chickens, is designed for kids, but you'll find plenty of adults without kids enjoying it, too.

South of Pescadero on CA 1 is one of the coast's must-see attractions: **Ano Nuevo State Reserve** (800-444-4445; www.parks.ca.org), where hundreds of elephant seals mate and give birth from December through March. They can be seen year-round, but during the mating period, bulls weighing up to five thousand pounds engage in noisy battles on the sand dunes as they fight over the females, making those four months peak visiting times. From mid-December through March, docents lead 3-mile walks and share their in-depth knowledge of the seals' lives and the area's natural history. (Advance reservations are necessary; see the reserve's contact information.) It is a flat, easy walk to the windswept point where the mating grounds are, but you should wear good walking shoes and layered clothing and brace yourself against the cold ocean air. For a longer hike, with views of the mating grounds and more bluffs, take the Ano Nuevo Point Trail, a 4.1-mile partial loop from the southwest corner of the park's parking lot.

A crab fisherman in Half Moon Bay's harbor

The garden at Half Moon Bay's Mill Rose Inn

Adjacent to the lot is the park's visitors center, which describes the area's marine life and history.

WHERE TO EAT

Half Moon Bay has only 16,000 residents, but the number and quality of its restaurants befits a town triple its size. **Pasta Moon** (315 Main St.; 650-726-5126; www.pastamoon.com) offers some the best Italian dishes in the region. **Cetrella** (845 Main St.; 650-726-4090; www.cetrella.com) is an elegant, highly rated restaurant with seasonal, Mediterranean cuisine. The more casual, European-style **Moonside Bakery and Cafe** (604 Main St.; 650-726-9070; www.moonsidebakery.com) serves sandwiches made from its own fresh bread. **Tres Amigos** (200 N. Cabrillo Hwy.; 650-726-6080) is a laid-back taqueria with authentic Mexican fare.

The harbor just north of town has a number of fish eateries, including **Sam's Chowder House**, (4210 N. Cabrillo Hwy.; 650-712-0245; www.samschowderhouse.com), which specializes in crab and grilled fish; it features oceanside dining and a handsome cocktail area. **Half Moon Bay Brewing Company** (390 Capistrano Way; 650-728-2739; www.hmbbrewingco.com) serves pints of beer on a heated patio overlooking the harbor. **Mezza Luna** (459 Prospect Way; 650-728-8108; www.mezzalunabythesea.com) is a lovely restaurant serving delicious pasta and other Italian specialties.

Duarte's Tavern (202 Stage Rd., Pescadero; 650-879-0464; www.duartestavern.com), an old, pine-paneled saloon and restaurant, has been a longtime favorite on the coast. Try one of the stellar soups—either cream of artichoke or cream of green chile (some get an order of both and mix them, which is delicious)—accompanied by warm sourdough bread. Then order a slice of the justifiably famous olallieberry pie for dessert.

WHERE TO SLEEP

There is a wide range of places to spend the night in the Half Moon Bay area, starting with budget lodging at two of the most picturesque hostels around. The **Point Montara Lighthouse** (650-728-7177; www.norcalhostels.org/montara) was established as a fog-signal station in 1875. It has a kitchen that guests use to prepare their own meals, dormitory-style bedrooms (by gender), and a private room. Reservations for a stay at the lighthouse should be made well in advance. Within walking distance is the **Fitzgerald Marine Reserve**, a 4-mile shore where starfish, crabs, mussels, sea anemones, and other fascinating marine life are exposed at low tide.

South of Half Moon Bay, near Ano Nuevo State Reserve and its elephant-seal grounds, is **Pigeon Point** (650-879-0633; 888-464-4872, ext. 73; www.norcalhostels .org/pigeon), another lighthouse turned hostel. The stately lighthouse, which has guided sailors since 1872, is a much photographed spot on a particularly jagged piece of coastline. There are private rooms, dorm rooms by gender, and a kitchen for general use.

For more luxury try the **Beach House Inn** (4100 N. Cabrillo Hwy.; 650-712-0220, 800-315-9366; www.beach-house.com), which has become a harbor landmark for its Nantucket-style architecture. Rooms have kitchenettes, fireplaces, and sitting rooms.

Those with oceanfront balconies are about $50 more a night, but are a nice splurge.

More intimate is the **Mill Rose Inn** (615 Mill St.; 650-726-8750, 800-900-7673; www.millroseinn .com), a frilly Victorian home from the late 1800s. Lush gardens of roses and other flowering plants surround the house and its four-room annex just a block from Main Street. Complimentary brandy and sherry are stocked in the rooms, and a lavish champagne breakfast is served either in your room or dining room. The private and comfy Briar Room is a guest favorite; the Baroque Room is the best value.

▌▌▌▌ LOCAL CONTACT

Half Moon Bay Coastside Chamber of Commerce and Visitors Bureau, 650-726-8380, www.half moonbaychamber.org.

27 · LOS GATOS & SARATOGA

Los Gatos is 60 miles south of San Francisco. From San Francisco, take I-280 to CA 85 south and then CA 17 south to the Los Gatos exit.

Los Gatos, a sunny, tree-lined town at the foot of the Santa Cruz Mountains, has a small-town atmosphere, but it isn't quite Mayberry. The average household income is $212,000, and top executives from the world's major high-tech companies make their homes here.

For most of its modern history, the town—whose name means "the cats," from the mountain lions seen by the first European settlers—was not affluent but merely a rail hub surrounded by fruit and almond orchards. (Rail lines went over the mountains to Santa Cruz and down the valley to Santa Clara.) Victorian houses and Craftsman bungalows from these old days line the neat blocks around downtown. In the later 20th century, Los Gatos morphed from a busy farm and train town into quiet bedroom community. It took off as a destination in the 1990s, when it became a hub of dining and shopping and a quaint refuge in sprawling Silicon Valley.

The tree-lined, leafy downtown, with its attractive town plaza, is a good place to explore on foot, especially if you like to shop: it's full of high-end stores. These include particularly inviting home décor shops, such as **Trent Pottery and Tile** (300 N. Santa Cruz Ave.) and **Domus** (40 N. Santa Cruz Ave.), which are unique and fun even if shopping is not your thing. From 8 AM to 1 PM on Sunday, year-round, the plaza bustles with a farmers' market.

Los Gatos' oldest building is the 1880 **Forbes Mill Annex**, which houses the town's history museum (75 Church St.; 408-395-7375; www.losgatosmuseum .org). There you can see exhibits about the past and pick up brochures for a self-guided historic walking tour.

For a pleasant stroll, walk the Los Gatos Creek Trail north from one of its downtown entrance point (the Plaza at Miles Avenue is one entrance point; the junction of Main Street and Forbes Hill is another). Follow the trail about a mile to **Vasona Lake County Park**, a beautiful oasis that includes a lake with paddleboats and rowboats to rent. Adjacent to the county park is **Oak Meadow Park**, where you'll find the **Bill Jones Wildcat Railroad**, an old

The Hotel Los Gatos and Dio Deka restaurant

train that kids love. The playground is also home to a restored 1915 carousel, originally built for San Francisco's Panama-Pacific International Exposition.

For a 2-mile hike with views of the valley, take the Los Gatos Creek Trail south toward the **Lexington Reservoir**. Near the reservoir dam are sites for fishing and picnicking; sorry, there's no swimming at the reservoir.

If you've ever wanted to connect to your inner *paisano* and try your hand at bocce—the Italian bowling game—you may find no better place than Los Gatos' **Campo Di Bocce** (565 University Ave.; 408-395-7650; www.campodibocce.com). The courtside Italian restaurant allows guests to watch the action while having lunch or dinner. There's a two-person minimum for renting a court during the day and a four-person minimum during the evening. The fee is $10 per bowler for one and a half hours.

For a more adventuresome outing, drive out of Los Gatos on CA 9, past Saratoga and into the Santa Cruz Mountains, to Skyline Boulevard (CA 35) and **Castle Rock State Park** (15000 Skyline Blvd.; 408-867-2952; www.parks.ca.gov). Here are spectacular sandstone formations that rock climbers use for practice. Walk the Saratoga Gap Trail through tall groves of firs and oaks. The 5.2-mile loop covers some steep terrain but leads to views of Castle Rock Falls, the Pacific Ocean, and sandstone outcroppings shaped and hollowed by the wind. An easier, 2-mile trail starts at Sempervirens Point and meanders through flower-filled Summitt Meadows. Trail maps are available at the park entrance.

Saratoga, another affluent Silicon Valley town nestled in the base of the Santa Cruz Mountains, is a quieter than Los Gatos and also has its own charms. Lots of antiques shops and boutiques can be found along its main thoroughfare. Just a mile from Saratoga is **Hakone Gardens** (21000 Big Basin Way; 408-741-4994; www.hakone.com), the oldest Japanese residential gardens in the western hemisphere. The grounds, where scenes from the 2005 movie *Memoirs of a Geisha* were filmed, include two traditional Japanese houses.

Near Saratoga is the reason many Bay Area people know the place: **Mountain Winery** (1483 Pierce Rd.; 408-741-2822; www.mountainwinery.com), home of Paul Masson wines and a beautiful outdoor concert arena where, among others, Willie Nelson, Norah Jones, and Diana Krall have performed. Dinner and concert packages are available. The winery, which has beautiful views of Santa Clara Valley, is open for tasting, and you can tour the historic building and its 12th-century Spanish portal.

Between Los Gatos and Saratoga, along CA 9, lies another popular concert venue: the **Villa Montalvo Arts Center** (408-961-5800; www.montalvoarts.org), a former estate transformed to art and culture haven. Concerts are performed on the front lawn of the stunningly grand villa or in the intimate carriage house. The center presents 100 concerts each year, featuring jazz, blues, rock,

and classical music from both established and up-and-coming artists. On nonconcert days, visitors come simply to stroll the center's 175 acres of hiking trails and gardens.

■■■■ WHERE TO EAT

La Boulanger (145 N. Main St.; 408-395-1344), a casual spot on the plaza, is perfect for a sandwich or coffee and dessert. Pick up picnic supplies or eat in at **Los Gatos Gourmet** (109 W. Main St., 408-354-5440; www.losgatos gourmet.com), a cozy place with a selection of artisan cheeses, wine, and sandwiches. Even if your sweet tooth isn't throbbing, poke around the delightful **Icing on the Cake** (50 W. Main St.; 408-354-2464; www.icingonthe cakebakery.com). The chocolate-buttermilk cake put the bakery on the map, but the cupcakes get raves, too. It also offers a fun selection of dessert plates and cards for sale.

Dio Deka (210 E. Main St.; 408-354-7700; www.diodeka.com) has risen to the top among Greek restaurants in the Bay Area. It's a beautiful, elegant room in the Hotel Los Gatos (see "Where to Sleep"). Among the most popular menu items are the lamb dishes, including the herb-crusted lamb chops and the slow-roasted lamb shoulder with ouzo, garlic confit, olives, and shaved Greek cheese. **Steamer's Grillhouse** (31 University Ave.; 408-395-2722; www.steamers-restaurant.com) specializes in seafood and grilled meats and serves pizzas from a stone oven; it also has a lively cocktail lounge and an oyster bar that serves seafood appetizers.

No discussion of local restaurants would be complete without a mention of **Manresa** (320 Village Ln., 408-354-4330; www.manresa restaurant.com), a Michelin two-star restaurant that is considered one of the top in the U.S. The menu's highlights are its creative, French-inspired dishes made with local produce, including vegetables from the restaurant's garden. Advance reservations are advised.

Saratoga also has many fine restaurants, including **Sent Sovi** (14583 Big Basin Way; 408-867-3110), which serves contemporary French cuisine. **Lupretta's Deli** (14480 Big Basin Way; 408-484-0004) is an institution and famous for its raviolis and meatball sandwiches. **Blue Rock Shoot Cafe** (14523 Big Basin Way; 408-872-0309) is a woodsy hangout serving salads, coffee, and desserts indoors and out.

▪▪▪▪ WHERE TO SLEEP

Hotel Los Gatos (210 E. Main St.; 408-335-1700, 800-738-7477; www.jdvhotels.com) is a resort-like, luxurious hotel with a Mediterranean atmosphere. All rooms have separate showers and deep soaking tubs. The swimming pool and spa add to resort feel. The hotel is a pleasant 10-minute walk from downtown. **Toll House** (140 S. Santa Cruz Ave.; 408-395-7070, 800-238-6111; www.toll hous, the hotel.com), in the middle of Los Gatos, on the plaza, has the feel of an upscale business traveler's hotel. Renovated in 2004, it makes a nice weekend retreat, especially since it's steps away from all the shops and restaurants in town. Live jazz can be heard in the Three Degrees cocktail lounge.

In Saratoga, you'll find **the Inn at Saratoga** (20645 Fourth St., 408-867-5020; www.innatsaratoga.com). The décor is a bit 1980s and has lots of brass fixtures, but the large rooms and the location in the middle of town make up for lack of hip style. Reserve one of the rooms that have balconies overlooking bucolic Saratoga Creek. This hotel fills fast when Mountain Winery has a concert, so book well in advance.

▪▪▪▪ LOCAL CONTACT

Los Gatos Chamber of Commerce, visitors center at 349 N. Santa Cruz Ave.; 408-354-9300; www.losgatosweb.com. **Saratoga Chamber of Commerce**, 408-867-0753; www.saratogachamber.org.

28 · SANTA CRUZ

Santa Cruz is 70 miles south of San Francisco. Follow directions to Los Gatos (chapter 27) and continue on CA 17 south. Or, for a longer, scenic drive along the coast, follow directions for Half Moon Bay (chapter 26) and continue south on CA 1.

Some call **Santa Cruz** the quintessential California beach town, but the label doesn't quite fit. After all, there's a university (University of California Santa Cruz) that eschews organized sports (its mascot is the banana slug), and residents are a mix of Silicon Valley commuters, artists, hippies, and political radicals. A local bumper sticker insists, "Keep Santa Cruz weird." On the other hand, while other California beach towns claim to be surfing paradises, Santa Cruz is where Hawaiian royalty actually introduced the sport to the mainland.

The town's biggest attraction is a blast from the past: a classic cotton-candy-and-corn-dog amusement park, the **Santa Cruz Beach Boardwalk**, which celebrated its 100th year in 2007. It's a thrill to look up and see the thundering wooden roller coaster, the Giant Dipper, powered by the original 1924 engine, carrying clench-fisted riders through twists and turns. Many rides have been added over the decades (the Hurricane metal coaster and Logger's Revenge water ride, among them), but the Giant Dipper is still the boardwalk's major draw. For the faint of heart, there are other attractions, including Neptune's Kingdom, a two-story miniature-golf course with robotics, fiber optics, and special effects, and three arcades with vintage mechanical marvels and modern video games. The boardwalk's 1911 carousel has its original 72 hand-carved horses, two chariots, and a 342-pipe band organ. Admission to the boardwalk (400 Beach St.; 831-423-5590; www.beachboardwalk .com) is free, including on Friday nights in summertime, when oldies bands give concerts on the mile-long sandy beach.

The old wharf, a few hundred feet from the boardwalk, is lined with several old-style fish restaurants (Stagnaro Brothers has been there since 1937) and kitschy souvenir shops selling boatloads of seashell necklaces. It is worth a walk just for the views, particularly at sunset. For even better sightseeing, rent a kayak and paddle out to the nearby kelp forest to observe sea otters, harbor seals, maybe dolphins, and, during migrating months, gray whales. Guided tours and kayak rentals are available on the wharf from **Venture Quest** (2 Santa Cruz Wharf; 831-427-2267; www.kayak santacruz.com) or, about a mile south of town, at the Santa Cruz harbor, from **Kayak Connection** (413 Lake Ave.; 831-479-1121; www .kayakconnection.com).

You can also spot marine life from the beautiful, winding, paved path atop West Cliff Drive, just south of Santa Cruz beach. Walk the path or rent bicycles from **Electric Sierra Cycles** (302 Pacific Ave.; 831-425-1593; www .electricbikes.com), a block from the wharf. The company rents both regular bicycles and electric scooters and bikes that can zip along at 20 miles per hour. While cruising the path, stop at the **Santa Cruz Surfing Museum** (701 West Cliff Dr.; 831-420-6119; www .santacruzsurfingmuseum.org) in the **Mark Abbott Memorial Lighthouse**, named for a surfer who rode his last wave nearby. The museum houses a gift shop, displays of old surfboards (including some made of red-

wood planks), and shows videos about the sport.

The West Cliff Drive path eventually leads to **Natural Bridges State Park** (831-423-4609; www .parks.ca.gov), about 2½ miles south of Santa Cruz beach. Natural Bridges is a dramatic spot to watch sea otters, seals, and migrating whales. Along the beach are tidepools full of sea stars and sea anemones. From mid-October through the end of February, a main attraction here is the park's **Monarch Butterfly Natural Preserve**, where 100,000 butterflies spend the winter, clustered for warmth on the trees. A demonstration patch with monarch eggs and caterpillars, a picnic area, and a visitors center with natural history information all make visiting the preserve a worthwhile outing.

To really get you into the Santa Cruz vibe, **Club Ed** (831-464-0177, 800-287-7873;www.club-ed.com) offers surfing lessons and rentals. It is run by the head instructor for the UC Santa Cruz surfing program, whose grandmother was taught in 1915 by legendary Hawaiian surfing masters. Or you could look into the school run by Richard Schmidt, another veteran surfer (849 Almar Ave.; 831-423-0928; www.richardschmidt.com).

If you haven't been to **downtown Santa Cruz** in 10 years or

The Santa Cruz Beach Boardwalk

ROBERT HOLMES/ CALTOUR

more, you are in for a surprise. Spruced up since it was damaged in the 1989 Loma Prieta earthquake, it has some nicely refurbished businesses (even the Starbucks here doesn't look like a chain). The main thoroughfare is no longer called the Pacific Garden Mall (people kept looking for a modern "mall") but simply Pacific Avenue. There's plenty of evidence that you are in self-proclaimed Surf City, such as the O'Neill Surf Shop and Pacific Wave store standing side by side on the avenue. At Cooper and Pacific is an only-in–Santa Cruz shop: Gelatomania, an oxygen bar and ice cream parlor that has 50 flavors of ice cream, made by local Buddhist monks.

With its large college student population, Santa Cruz has a lively nightlife. The **Kuumbwa Jazz Center** (320-2 Cedar St.; 831-427-2227; www.kuumbwajazz.org) is a nonprofit organization dedicated to promoting jazz and other musical genres with nightly performances. **The Catalyst** (1011 Pacific Ave.; 831-423-1338; www .catalystclub.com), with its 5,000 square feet of dance space, draws acts from around the world. Pick up copies of two free weeklies, *Good Times* and *Metro*, for club and event listings.

A few miles south of Santa Cruz is **Capitola**, a 150-year old beach town that really comes alive on summer weekends. (The traffic can be terrible, so plan ahead; the visitors guide devotes an entire page to parking.) On Labor Day weekend the town celebrates its claim to fame—the begonia, the flower that was hybridized here—with a parade and festival. Take a walk along the wharf and esplanade, check out the beach-volleyball action and the Crayola-colored beach bungalows, and cross the bridge over the San Lorenzo River, which meets the Pacific here.

▪▪▪▪ WHERE TO EAT

Among the restaurants of note in Santa Cruz's downtown is **Aqua Blue** (1108 Pacific Ave.; 831-423-6999), a sushi bar and California/Asian fusion specialist. Locals also love breakfast at **Zachary's** (819 Pacific Ave.; 831-427-0646) for its omelettes, pancakes, and coffee cake. **Lulu Carpenter** (1545 Pacific Ave.; 831-429-9804) is a handsome, European-style coffeehouse with healthy lunch options. There may be no better place for picnic supplies than **Zoccoli's** (1534 Pacific Ave; 831-423-1711; www.zoccolis.com), an Italian-style deli with a big selection of sandwiches and salads. **Taqueria Vallarta** (1101 Pacific Ave.; 831-471-2655), casual and inexpensive, serves above-average tacos, burritos, and seafood specialties.

In Capitola, the **Paradise Beach Grille** (215 Esplanade; 831-476-4900; wwwparadisebeachgrille.com), known for its lively cocktail bar, offers a signature dish: halibut wrapped in thin slices of potatoes and topped in beurre blanc sauce. For more elegant dining, there's the romantic favorite, **Shadowbrook** (1750 Wharf Rd.; 831-475-1511; www.shadowbrook-capitola.com),

perched on a hill overlooking the Pacific and accessible by cable car or footpath.

▪▪▪▪ WHERE TO SLEEP

Santa Cruz has dozens of chain hotels and motels and a few boutique-style accommodations. **The Adobe on Green Street** (103 Green St.; 831-469-9866; www .adobeongreen.com) is tucked in a neighborhood that feels miles from downtown but is only about a five-minute walk away. Built in 1947, the house was constructed during a renaissance in adobe homes. The four rooms are quiet, and their bathrooms are lined in Mexican tiles. There's a lovely living room, library/computer room, gardens, and patios.

The **West Cliff Inn** (174 West Cliff Dr.; 800-979-0910; www.west cliffinn.com) opened in summer of 2007 on the bluff overlooking the beach and boardwalk. The three-story Victorian, built in 1877 as a private home, has a wraparound porch and nine luxurious rooms, each with a fireplace and marble bathroom. The décor is in crisp blues and whites and includes rattan furnishings.

Pleasure Point Inn (2-3665 East Cliff Dr.; 831-475-4657; www.pleasurepointinn.com) is a surfer's dream home, situated on a cliff overlooking the Pacific, more than a mile from downtown. The four guest rooms are large, and each has a private entrance. The huge deck on the roof features a hot tub and chaise lounges. Return guests get 15 percent off rates.

Capitola's **Inn at Depot Hill** (250 Monterey Ave.; 831-462-3376; 800-572-2632; www.innsbythe sea.com) is one of the most luxurious hotels in the entire county. The rooms are sumptuous. Two, Portofino and Sissinghurst, have private garden patios, fireplaces, and marble bathrooms. Nearby is

Monarch Cove Inn (620 El Salto Dr., Capitola; 831-464-1295; www .monarch-cove-inn.com), which not as lavish but has gorgeous views of Monterey Bay from several rooms. Expansive gardens invite guests to linger and listen to the waves crashing below.

▌▌▌▌ LOCAL CONTACT

Santa Cruz Conference and Visitors Council, visitors center at 1211 Ocean St., 800-833-3494; www.santacruz.org.

HEADING SOUTH:

100 Miles and More from San Francisco

The Big Sur Coast

ROBERT HOLMES/CALTOUR

29 • THE MONTEREY PENINSULA

Monterey is 110 miles south of San Francisco off CA 1. Follow the directions to Santa Cruz (chapter 28) and take CA 1 south.

Many of us imagine the **Monterey Peninsula** as glamorous—multi-millionaires, celebrities, swanky hotels, emerald green fairways at some of the world's most exclusive golf courses. If you limit yourself to certain areas, it is indeed posh. But there's much more to this peninsula.

For one, it is, in a sense, the West Coast version of Jamestown or Plymouth Rock. The first European to land here, Sebastian Vizcaina, arrived in 1602 and claimed the land for Spain. The city of Monterey later became the Spanish and Mexican capital of California and the first capital of the American state. As you roam downtown you'll see many whitewashed adobe-brick buildings that evoke the Spanish-Mexican era.

Monterey's main thoroughfare, Alvarado Street, leads out from the **Custom House Plaza**, where markers indicate spots for the park's Path of History self-guided tour. The 10 buildings on this easy stroll, all part of the **Monterey State Historic Park** (831-649-7118; www.parks.ca.gov,

www.historicmonterey.org), include the Custom House, dating from 1827 and its interior rooms looking as they did in that year; California's First Theater, built in 1846; and, most interesting, **Colton Hall Museum** on Pacific Street between Jefferson and Madison, where California's first constitution was drafted in 1849 amid heated debates about slavery (outlawed) and the state's eastern boundary (the Rocky Mountains were at one point considered). Before voting, each resolution was translated into Spanish, still the native language of most *Californios*.

Another look into early California can be seen at the **Cooper-Molera Adobe** (525 Polk St.; 831-649-7111; www.parks.ca.gov). The home was built in the 1830s by John Rogers Cooper, a ship's captain from New England who married into the Molera family, prominent early settlers from Mexico. You can take a self-guided tour of the house and the two-acre yard, a re-creation of the farm and gardens of the time. Forty-five-minute guided tours are conducted every day except Thursday. Inside the house, the Cooper Museum Store sells reproductions of toys and household goods of the mid-1800s and has a good selection of books on California history.

History buffs also will enjoy the **Monterey Maritime Museum** (5 Custom House Plaza; 831-375-1643; www.montereyhistory.org), which houses exhibits on the rich seafaring and naval history of the area and is illuminated by the Fresnel lens from the old Point Sur Light.

On the waterfront, **Cannery Row** is mostly shops and restaurants now, but sea lions still bark noisily, sea otters float belly up, and seagulls and pelicans wheel overhead; you can almost imagine what it was like when the sardine boats pulled up on one side, the freight trains shuttled along the other, and the big canneries hummed in between.

One of these former canneries is now occupied by the **Monterey Bay Aquarium** (886 Cannery Row; 831-648-4800; www.montereybay aquarium.org). You can spend the day at the aquarium, but if you have only a couple of hours, one of the highlights is the three-story kelp forest, open to the sky. Twice a day, a diver feeds fish in the kelp forest while talking to the audience via underwater

microphone, explaining this re-creation the aquatic world of Monterey Bay, one of the richest marine environments on the planet. Another must-see is the two-story sea-otter display, where the agile animals can be viewed through plate glass as they zip through the water; feeding shows are scheduled twice a day.

The town next to Monterey, **Pacific Grove**, has an entirely different atmosphere than its Spanish-influenced neighbor. This seaside town, founded by Methodists as a religious retreat center in 1875, has a more buttoned-up, New England ambiance. The town is lovely for strolling, and it is quiet—a quality that is probably a by-product of its decades-long ban on alcohol, which was not lifted until 1969. Lover's Point Beach on Ocean View Boulevard is a must, particularly at sunset in April and May, when a type of ice plant known locally at as the "Pacific Grove magic carpet" blossoms in a burst of hot pink on the hillside above the beach.

Lover's Point is the start of the **Monterey Bay Coastal Trail**, a walking and biking path that stretches north from Pacific Grove about 18 miles. Much of what's on the trail you'd never see by car, including the high sand dunes of the decommissioned Fort Ord.

Adventures by the Sea (831-372-1807; www.adventuresbythesea.com), which has several locations in Pacific Grove, Pebble Beach, and Monterey, rents bikes. The trail is packed on weekends in the Cannery Row area, making bicycling slow going, so a good bet is to rent a bike in Pacific Grove and ride south through Lover's Point to Pebble Beach—an 11-mile trip along some of the most spectacular parts of California. South of Pacific Grove the coastal trail ends, but bike lanes and wide shoulders allow easy riding, including along 17-Mile Drive.

Long one of the most popular routes on the peninsula, **17-Mile Drive** is a private toll road—free to bicyclists and walkers—maintained by the Pebble Beach Company (800-654-9300; www.pebblebeach.com). Enter by one of five gates and enjoy the drive as it winds through the Del Monte Forest and along the coast, past opulent mansions and the Pebble Beach and Spanish Bay golf courses. The entrance fee of $9 per car includes a map of the scenic spots, including **the Lone Cypress**, a much-photographed 200-year-old tree that grows out of an oceanside rock outcropping.

To the immediate south of Monterey is cute-as-a-button **Carmel-by-the-Sea**. Almost precious in its charm, this town once was a flourishing artists' colony, though few artists can afford to live here today. Still, the number of art galleries (90) along Carmel's Ocean Avenue and side streets must be higher per capita than anywhere else in the country. The 1-square-mile village has some quaint laws, such as those saying houses must have no street addresses (homes go simply by their streets or names such as Periwinkle or Tinker Bell) and that there are to be no sidewalks and no streetlights in town. The village's beauty comes, in part, from its towering pine trees and spectacular white sand beach at the foot of Ocean Avenue.

Carmel is also home to the sec-

Lover's Point, Pacific Grove

Golf at Pebble Beach

ond Spanish mission built in California. San Carlos Borromeo de Carmelo, known simply as the **Carmel Mission** (3080 Mission Rd.; 831-624-3600; www.carmel mission.org), was built in 1797 of local stone and is the burial site of Father Junipero Serra, the founder of the mission chain. The cell where Serra died and the original mission library are among the rooms open for visits.

Three miles south of Carmel is **Point Lobos State Reserve** (831-624-4909; www.pointlobos.org), which lives up to its title as the "crown jewel" of the California state parks system. The crashing waves, the unbelievable shades of green, blue, and turquoise water, and the wind-blown Monterey pines may seem familiar, as Point Lobos was photographed by Ansel Adams and used as a dramatic background in movies such as Alfred Hitchcock's *Rebecca*.

Stop at the reserve's entrance gate and chat with the ranger to find the best areas to explore; the season may dictate where you want to go. You may meet Ranger Chuck Bancroft, who has spent 26 years at Point Lobos and says he still hasn't seen it all. He recommends that first-timers park at the main lot and walk the ¾-mile Cypress Grove Trail. The trail winds through one of only two groves of naturally growing Mon-

terey cypresses on earth before emerging from the trees to reveal stunning views of Carmel Bay. Then you can drive or walk a mile to the Bird Island parking lot and take the ¾-mile loop trail through the woods to a pair of jade green coves with white sand beaches, accessible by long staircases. You'll pass wildflowers and look down on Bird Island, which in spring and summer attracts cormorants in the thousands. Sea otters play in the kelp beds, and harbor seals bask on the rocks.

▪ ▪ ▪ ▪ WHERE TO EAT

In Monterey, for breakfast or lunch, try **Loulou's Griddle in the Middle** (Municipal Wharf; 831-372-0568) an old shack whose paint job—canary yellow with bright red trim—is as charming as its name. Sand dabs, calamari, and other local fish are served in big portions on bright red plates; as you dine, you view the more touristy Monterey wharf across a sea of sailboats. **Monterey's Fish House** (2114 Del Monte Ave.; 831-373-4647), though on a busy boulevard with no ocean views, has some of the best seafood around. Try the petrale sole, calamari, and the oysters. This local favorite fills up fast.

Downtown, try **Rosine's** (434 Alvarado St.; 831-375-1400; www .rosinesmonterey.com), which has towering layer cakes that will make your sweet tooth quiver, and the **Monterey Cafe** (489 Alvarado St.; 831-646-1021), a busy, old-fashioned eatery where pecan-banana pancakes are a specialty. **Turtle Bay Taqueria** (431 Tyler St.; 831-333-1500; www .fishwife.com) is a fun, casual place with tasty grilled fish tacos and healthy Mexican dishes.

Passionfish in Pacific Grove (701 Lighthouse Ave.; 831-655-3311; www.passionfish.net) is a highly touted restaurant where you'll feel good about what you're eating: all the seafood is "sustainable"—raised or caught with minimal impact on the environment. **The Fishwife at Asilomar** (1996½ Sunset Dr.; 831-375-7108; www.fishwife.com) specializes in local seafood with a spicy Caribbean influence and serves it with local produce from the Salinas Valley.

For breakfast or lunch in Carmel, **Katy's Place** (Mission St. between Fifth and Sixth avenues; 831-624-0199; www.katysplace carmel.com) serves big portions from an international menu that includes everything from huevos rancheros to Swedish pancakes, as well as American chow.

▪▪▪▪ WHERE TO SLEEP

In downtown Monterey, **Casa Munras** (700 Munras Ave.; 800-222-2446; www.hotelcasamunras .com), built around an 1824 hacienda, is a good choice because of its central location. Forty-six of its 166 rooms have fireplaces and sitting areas.

In Pacific Grove, the **Gosby House** (643 Lighthouse Ave.; 831-375-1287, 800-234-1425; www .foursisters.com) is a flower- and antiques-filled bed-and-breakfast. Room 13 is especially lovely with its king-sized bed, gas fireplace, and private patio with porch swing. Room 2, with a big corner bay window, costs less than other rooms because its bathroom (not shared) is across the hall.

Standing out in Carmel is **Tradewinds** (Mission St. at Third Ave.; 831-624-2776, 800-624-6665; www.tradewindsinn.com), a luxurious inn with tranquil Asian-inspired décor. Rooms have sumptuous linens and slate bathrooms; kimonos are provided.

Carmel's **Cypress Inn** (Lincoln and Seventh Ave.; 800-443-7443; www.cypress-inn.com) takes four-legged guests. The owner is none other than Doris Day, who turned the Spanish-Mediterranean inn into a pet-friendly hotel. An estimated 50 percent of guests bring their dogs. (Carpets in their accommodations are deep cleaned after checkout; still, this inn is recommended for allergy sufferers.) Rooms in the new 12-room annex are much prettier and pricier than those in the original building. Even if you don't stay here, come in for a drink at Terry's Bar (named after Doris's late son, Terry Melcher), look at the movie posters, and perhaps catch an old Doris Day-Rock Hudson movie on the big-screen TVs.

The closest hotel to the beach in Carmel is **the Colonial Terrace** (San Antonio St. and 13th Ave.; 831-624-2741, 800-345-8220; www.thecolonialterrace.com), located in a gorgeous residential neighborhood a few steps from the beach. Each of the 28 rooms is unique in layout and décor. Seven have ocean views. Room 21B has a balcony and fireplace.

▮▮▮▮ LOCAL CONTACT

Monterey County Convention and Visitors Bureau, visitors centers in El Estero Park at Franklin and Camino El Estero and at 150 Olivier St.; 888-221-1010; www.montereyinfo.org. **Pacific Grove Chamber of Commerce**, visitors center at corner of Central and Forest avenues, 800-656-6650, www.pacificgrove.org. **Carmel Chamber of Commerce**, visitors center on San Carlos between Fifth and Sixth; 800-550-4333; www.carmelcalifornia.org.

30 · BIG SUR

Big Sur is 150 miles south of San Francisco and 30 miles south of the Monterey Peninsula (see chapter 29) on CA 1.

With its miles and miles of gorgeous coastline, **Big Sur** has long been a magnet for artists and writers, who have made their individual attempts to capture its amazing beauty. The descriptions used, such as "the Greatest Meeting of Land and Sea" (now a slogan of sorts), may seem hyperbole until you start the drive south of Carmel on CA 1.

As it stretches 90 miles from Carmel to San Luis Obispo County, the road winds against the western flank of the Santa Lucia mountain range, mostly within sight of the Pacific Ocean. The ocean-and-mountain landscape is awesome. The climate is mild, but, as in most places on the California coast, chilly, foggy mornings (even in summer) turn into warm sunny afternoons, so dressing in layers is advised.

Thirteen miles south of Carmel is the most photographed spot along the route, the **Bixby Creek Bridge**, one of the world's highest single-span concrete arch bridges. From here on, you'll want to pull over often to enjoy the views and take photos.

Big Sur's coast is a prime area for viewing sea otters, harbor seals, sea lions, and whales. December through January, gray whales migrate south to their breeding grounds off the Baja California coast; March and April, they return north to their summer feeding grounds. Often, they are so close to shore you don't need binoculars to see them. Bird life is plentiful, as well, and includes marine varieties such as cormorants, gulls, sandpipers, and pelicans; geese, cranes, ducks and other waterfowl; and, in the forests, songbirds of many types. Soaring and swooping falcons and hawks are common sights, and you even may spot a California condor, North America's largest land bird.

Nineteen miles south of Carmel, **Point Sur Light Station** (831-625-4419; www.pointsur.org), part of Point Sur State Historic Park, has guided ships for more than 100 years. Today its operation is automated. Volunteers lead three-hour walking tours on a path less than a mile long but that has two stairways, the longest with 61 steps. The tours are limited to 40 people and offered on weekends year-round, plus on Wednesday from April through October, and, in July and August, on Thursday as well. In addition, moonlight tours are given from April through October on nights of the full moon.

Twenty miles south of Carmel, **Andrew Molera State Reserve** (Hwy. 1; 831-667-2315; www.parks .ca.gov) is a 4,800-acre swath of wilderness with meadows, oak and redwood groves, streams, and beaches. The highlights are the bluffs and secluded beaches. Horseback tours (831-625-5486; www.molerahorsebacktours.com), designed for inexperienced riders, saunter across the shallow Big Sur River to the beach. Or you can walk the easy, flat, 2-mile loop trail from the parking lot though meadows and trees, past the Cooper Cabin (the oldest pioneer structure in the region), to an an ocean vista and a beach strewn with driftwood. This state park, like others along the coast, charges a day-use fee. However, this fee covers entrance to other state parks on the same day, so be sure to keep the receipt.

At **Pfeiffer Big Sur State Park** (Big Sur Station #1; 831-667-2315; www.parks.ca.gov), 26 miles south of Carmel, stop at the ranger station and visitors center for maps and park information. An array of hiking trails await, including an easy, 1.4-mile round-trip along the Big Sur River that takes you past swimming holes and through redwood groves to a 60-foot-high waterfall. Buzzard's Roost is a moderate, 4.8-mile round-trip through redwood, oak, and bay trees to Pfeiffer Ridge, which affords impressive coastal views.

There is no incorporated town of Big Sur—only a tiny post office and some stores, shops, and gas stations along a 6-mile section of CA 1. Many of the businesses here do not have street addresses, because there's only one "street," and that's the highway.

A haven of bohemian literary culture is the **Henry Miller Memorial Library** (Hwy. 1; 831-667-2574; www.henrymiller.org), peaceful spot that is more like a writer's hangout than a library or a memorial. Visitors get a sense of the once-controversial author, who lived in Big Sur from 1944 to 1962, from the collection of memorabilia and his works, once considered so earthy that most were banned in this country. The library is a fine place to relax, and you can enjoy poetry readings, live music, and other events on the library's front lawn in summer. Nearby, the **Coast Gallery** (Hwy. 1; 831-667-2301; www.coastgalleries

.com), an extensive arts and crafts store with Henry Miller lithographs, is worth a stop.

Julia Pfeiffer Burns State Park, 37 miles south of Carmel on CA 1 (831-667-2315; www.parks.ca .gov), has some of the area's best hiking. An easy, 10-minute stroll takes you to the McWay Falls overlook, where an 80-foot waterfall drops from the cliffs to a lovely cove with white sand beach (that is, unfortunately, off limits). The terrace at the end of the overlook is all that remains of the Brown family home; the Brown family owned a ranch here and bequeathed it to the state for use as a park, dedicated to the memory of early pioneer Julia Pfeiffer Burns. The park's other trails wind through the redwood forest and along creeks. Ewoldsen, a 4½-mile round-trip loop trail, starts from the parking lot and climbs up through redwoods and fern-lined canyons to a ridge where you'll find spectacular coastal views.

Esalen (55000 Hwy. 1; 831-667-3005; www.esalen.org), the ground-breaking retreat dedicated to personal and social transformation, has grown into a Big Sur institution. Nonguests can experience its famous cliff-side, clothing-optional hot tubs two ways: by booking a massage, which allows use of the tubs, or

simply by making a reservation to use them between 1 and 3 AM. People in the know plan their trips to Big Sur around this magical, middle-of-the-night al fresco, au naturel soaking.

▪▪▪▪ WHERE TO EAT

Life may not get any better than lunch on a sunny day on the terrace at **Nepenthe** (Hwy. 1; 831-667-2345; www.nepenthebigsur .com), where Portobello or steak sandwiches are the specialties. Sunset cocktails round the big fire ring overlooking miles of coastline and ocean aren't bad, either. **Cafe Kevah** (see contact information for Nepenthe), on the same hill but below Nepenthe, also has great terrace views and serves a more basic, less expensive breakfast and lunch.

Big Sur Bakery and Restaurant (Hwy. 1; 831-667-0520; www .bigsurbakery.com), is the kind of place that has a "Resist Corporate Coffee" sticker on the espresso machine and Neil Young on its stereo. Its bread, baked in a wood-fired oven, is coveted all over the region. Brunch dishes, particularly the potato frittatas, are a specialty. **Deetjen's** restaurant (48865 Hwy. 1; 831-667-2377; www.deetjens.com) consists of four snug rooms with fireplaces, candlelight, and classical music accompanying meals. Eggs benedict is a breakfast favorite; dinner specials use fresh, local ingredients. On a cold day, when there's a warm fire crackling beside your table, you won't want to leave. **Cielo**, at the Ventana Inn (Hwy. 1; 831-667-4242; www.ventanainn .com), is a gorgeous, romantic restaurant. It features a 50-mile view from its dining terrace and an outdoor cocktail lounge that is ideal for either lunch or sunset cocktails.

▪▪▪▪ WHERE TO SLEEP

Deetjen's Big Sur Inn (see "Where to Eat") may not be for everyone: Its cabins with small rooms and paper-thin walls have no telephones or TVs. Nestled in a redwood forest, they may be too dark and rustic for some, but others will find them enchanting and comfy. The inn is the creation of Norwegian Helmuth Deetjen, who built each cabin to be wildly different in size and shape. The Creek House, with its big brick

fireplace, raises the bar on the concept of cozy.

Don't let the pedestrian exterior of the **Glen Oaks Motel** (Hwy. 1; 831-667-2105; glenoaksbigsur .com) discourage you. Inside are newly revamped rooms with Asian-inspired décor, slate floors in the bathrooms, and exposed brick walls. (The motel calls the rooms "post-adobe units.") Bed linens are organic cotton. These rooms cost less than most in Big Sur and less you'd expect for such stylish surroundings.

The **Big Sur River Inn's** (Hwy. 1 at Pheneger Creek; 831-667-2700; www.bigsurriverinn.com) selling points are its swimming and bucolic riverside location. Guests dangle their feet in the river as they relax in rattan chairs set in the gentle current. The room décor is nothing fancy, but the friendly staff and river setting make the inn pleasant enough. Only the two-room suites overlook the river; the other units are

Lunch on the terrace at Nepenthe

McWay Falls, Julia Pfeiffer Burns State Park

in a building across the highway.

A new experience on the coast here is **Treebones Resort** (71895 Hwy. 1; 877-424-4787; www.tree bonesresort.com), which opened in 2006 to glowing reviews. The resort offers luxury camping: 16 yurt tents perched on a ridge overlooking the Pacific; each has heating, a sink, and French doors leading to a deck. Yurt 15 is the most sought-after; secluded in a pine grove, it has a full ocean view. Bathrooms are in a common area. The inviting main lodge or the cliffside swimming pool, heated year-round, are good places to linger with a good book.

▮▮▮▮ LOCAL CONTACT

Big Sur Chamber of Commerce, 831-667-2100; www.bigsur california.org.

INDEX